HELEN ROCK'S IRISH GARDENING

For Rupert 'Victor' Rock

Helen Rock's

IRISH GARDENING

THE LILLIPUT PRESS

First published 1999 by
THE LILLIPUT PRESS LTD
62-63 Sitric Road, Arbour Hill,
Dublin 7, Ireland.

A CIP record for this
title is available from
The British Library.

ISBN 1 901866 24 6

Grateful acknowledgment is made to the editors of *The Sunday Tribune*,
where the contents of this book originally appeared
in somewhat different form.

Set in 11 on 14 Adobe Garamond
Printed in Ireland by ColourBooks of Baldoyle, Dublin

Contents

Contents

THE GARDENER'S CALENDAR

DESIGN & TACTICS

Planning a Front Garden

In the same way that people know you through your dog, those who have been walking past your garden every day for years build up a relationship with it – and through it their perception of you. The snowdrops, crocuses and early narcissi are the stars of my front garden, and while they're playing to the crowd I'm the good fairy of the neighbourhood.

There have been all sorts of interesting encounters over the snowdrops. Once a tired-looking man with a beautiful country voice knocked at the door and touchingly begged for just one to take away with him. He didn't know what they were called, he said, but the drifts reminded him of a happy time in his childhood. On the other hand, after the bearded irises bloom *en masse* in June, my front garden, overhung as it is with limes and planes, falls apart somewhat.

It is then that all the compliments stop. Instead you get silent glances of pity or scorn from your former admirers, because you've failed to live up to your early promise. Until the fragrant green and white snowdrops reappear to delight everybody, the damp squib that was your summer garden is forgiven, if not forgotten. But with the snowdrops comes a softening of the earth and a whole new year in which to build up a better garden.

It is a rare thing to have an open and sunny front garden near the centre of a city. Most of them are substantially shaded by buildings or masonry of one sort or another. They are generally sucked dry by the same masonry, and by shrubs and trees planted too close together in sour, arid soil that hasn't seen a nourishing compost or any but cat manure since around the time people got rid of the open fire and took chemical gardening to their bosoms.

The majority of front gardens consist of a rectangle or square of grass on one side of a path which leads in a straight or curved line from the gate to the door of the house. Perhaps there is also a narrow strip of soil running along the other side of the path. Trees and shrubs in your own or your neighbours' gardens create deeply shaded areas which narrow your chances of ever having a truly wonderful mixed border that will amaze the public all year round. These are the most problematic and challenging to design, not least because their success hinges on a harmonious relationship with neighbouring views on three sides.

If you live in a perfectly symmetrical, double-fronted house, making a good design is much easier. There are two ways you can go about it, formal and informal. For the simplest version of the former, all you need is a straight path as wide as the front step, running in a direct line from the gate to the hall door, and two more running under the windows at each side of the house.

The paths could be laid in flags, setts, gravel, brick or quartz-studded concrete, which weathers nicely, spurred on by an initial application of yoghurt or sour milk. Whatever material you use, the important thing is to make sure it complements the house but doesn't outshine it. To complete the perfectly formal effect all you need is two lawns bordered by low evergreen hedges in, say, box or yew. This simplest of plans will work beautifully all year round, even if you resist ever adding another note of colour. There are men all over the country who like clipping and mowing, so maintenance of this garden would be a dream for them.

A thrilling example of the informal way to do this sort of garden can be seen on the north side of Kenilworth Square in Dublin 6. The broad, chest-high iron gate to the left side of this perfectly proportioned house is arched over by a romantically trained fairy thorn coming from the right. On the left is an assortment of slightly tender and exotic shrubs and small trees. To see a bit more of this tantalizing place, one has to go up on tiptoe and peer through the arch of thorn.

One broad sweep describes the curve of a single path, wide enough for two people to walk companionably side by side. Though the path leads inevitably to the prettiest of doorways, there are distractions all along the way, with strong, structural planting softening the curve and screening out what lies beyond. Little unobtrusive patches of bare earth appear in different places as the seasons progress but are soon covered by good displays of bulbs and herbaceous stuff.

Even in the dead of winter this garden is friendly and exciting, full of atmosphere and capable of stirring the spirits of the jaded gardener. It's all very well, though, taking these two examples of perfect symmetry. Symmetry is easy to work with and it's difficult to go too far wrong when it is the deciding factor.

Most front gardens are not easy. Even if you go for a complete makeover and construct a wonderful scree garden, you've got to get it absolutely right from the start. But any progress is better than none at all, so see below for a description of a few good plants that will thrive in the polluted hearts of our big towns and cities.

❧ A box hedge needs a clip in spring and later in July, but don't leave it too late in the season or you will be left with rusty brown ends which will make the plant look shabby right through winter, until growth starts again. If buying enough box plants to make a decent hedge is beyond your means, and time is not a problem, then just buy two or three and take dozens of cuttings, which will be ready for planting out in a year.

❧ The glossy, shapely leaves of the Mexican orange blossom (*Choisya ternata*) go all the way down to the ground and look good all year round. It will grow in some of the most difficult places. In our temperate climate it often puts out its fragrant white flowers twice a year, in April and September. I wouldn't bother with the yellow-leaved version, 'Sundance'. Its colour is too persistent.

❧ In a sunny place, a big sprawling rosemary leaning over the wall or through the railings will delight passersby – as will lavender, though it will soon be picked clean. The shadows cast on walls and hard surfaces by the giant-leaved and amazingly tolerant *Fatsia japonica*, which has an extra season of interest in November when mad white bobbles appear, can be dramatic.

∽An evergreen Daphne, like the lovely *D. pontica*, has pale green flowers in May which take on a stunning lemony fragrance in the evenings. *Daphne tangutica*, another evergreen, flowers at the same time and again towards the end of summer. *D. odorais* has heavily scented flowers from February to April. All of these thrive on alkaline soil.

Two Urban Gardens

Now that the fashion for terraced period houses around Dublin is firmly established, proud new owners are often daunted by the question of what to do with the long, narrow strip of back garden that almost inevitably accompanies them. These houses don't come cheap and, having spent all your money getting rid of the damp, letting light into the dark Victorian sculleries and tying down the thatch, there's not enough left to bring in that wonderful garden designer you may have dreamt about hiring because you think you know nothing about gardening.

The secret of gardening is to start. Plants, by their nature, want to grow. Like people and animals, if you treat them well, give them plenty of food and drink, put them in positions that suit their sensitivities, keep them away from clashing companions but near others that have the same needs – and yes, talk to them – they will come up trumps. Design is another matter, and very personal.

Anne Ryder and Noel Buckley are next-door neighbours in Rathgar who illustrate this point very well. Both have narrow, formidably long (160-foot) town gardens with lowish stone walls running the entire length. Their tablecloth-sized front gardens face onto a heavily-treed private square, so the view from their drawing-room windows more or less takes care of itself. Neither has had any outside help and most of their plants, barring the fruits and bigger shrubs, have come from bits scrounged from other gardeners. They both used recycled bricks, stones and timber found in skips.

Anne has been gardening there for seven years and takes a semi-abstract, painterly approach. 'I am ruled by colours, by the plants themselves. Eventually, I want to create a controlled wilderness from just colour. My plants are survivors. I spend two months in the country every summer with the children, so they have to be. What's alive when I come back is alive.' Big, red oriental poppies ('It's a child's garden, really') now dominate the lush planting in the raised fifty-foot twin borders she has made at the bottom.

The shaded yard, screened by sweet-smelling *Philadelphus* and roses, is underplanted by old-fashioned *Campanula*, bulbs and a sweep of Japanese anemones. This opens out unexpectedly into a sunny herb and fruit garden where pears, apples, plums, roses and perennials make the perfect setting for a contemplative arbour. A simple path of grey stone and shingle meanders through this haven, and always the eye is led on to the explosion of colour in the herbaceous borders.

As you step down, these borders rise up around you, full with lilies, scented evening primrose from the Shackleton garden, hardy geraniums, *Kniphofia*, tall and short irises, honeysuckles, mounds of mossy saxifrages and rock roses. Gooseberries trained as standards, fruiting currants and raspberries, a fig tree and a magnificent young Morello cherry help complete the picture and send the senses reeling. Tucked away at the very end is another seating area, a glasshouse crammed with tomatoes and hundreds of young deciduous trees, including Roman oaks, Spanish chestnut, walnut, beech, hornbeam, fruiting quinces and maritime pines that Anne has grown from seed to plant in her few acres of bogland in Co. Sligo.

When Noel moved in next door three years ago, he inherited an old red climbing rose, a golden privet, a long hedge of *Escallonia*, a small holly, a large apple tree which dominated the centre of a scraggy lawn, and a determined clan of bindweed with which he is still doing battle. A painter of formal landscapes and still lifes in his spare time, Noel's approach to the garden was dictated by the view he would have from his dining-room, which overlooks a dark, narrow yard.

His inspiration speeded along by Anne's gloriously informal planting next door, he set about constructing the bones of a formal garden, full of separate areas for different moods. The first thing he did was buttress the *Escallonia*, concealing the garden's boundaries from the windows and implying a theatrical proscenium arch beyond which could lie acres of lawn. Raised beds in the yard flourish with hostas and ferns; the sun-loving, evergreen *Clematis armandii* is amazingly healthy in a large pot at the back door, covers the drainpipes and lends a certain exotica; and *Macleaya cordata, Euphorbia wulfenii* and other shade-tolerant plants in pots and beds give way to the lawn.

This is a new garden: arches cut into the hedge wait for statuary and seating; a pergola waits for its new clothes of rose and clematis; a border of hot colours is growing up around the old red rose; the smoke bush, *Cotinus coggyria*, waits to rise and echo a mature copper beech three gardens away – and then suddenly you're out into what seems like a large square, cleverly constructed in staggered diagonals, a repetition of triangles and squares with raised levels, which is well on the road to being a very private, sun-soaked, formal Mediterranean garden planted with box edging, lavenders, santolinas and rues. Its walls will soon be clothed with heavenly white roses, jasmines, clematis and, not least, says Noel, 'pears for my heirs'.

Kniphofia

Planting under Deciduous Trees

At a party the other night a woman was talking about her weeping ash. She drew quite a crowd. This beautiful native tree, with its strong black winter skeleton and feathery summer foliage, was a giant, she said. She loved it and was keeping it, but she didn't like the way it dominated her smallish back garden, creating a large area of dry summer shade under which little would grow.

People nodded sympathetically, though in inheriting a mature ash she is actually quite lucky. Its airy foliage lets in more light and moisture than the usual deciduous trees planted in old town gardens, so her choice of planting can be drawn from a much broader woodland spectrum than if she was landed with a lime, plane or spreading horse chestnut.

The quest to give year-long interest to the ground under deciduous trees is one I embarked on some time ago. Ours is a railed front garden, completely dominated by a huge lime and an absolutely ancient plane, which were once part of a rather grand avenue of trees. In winter and spring, when the branches are bare, the ground beneath gets enough moisture to ensure that plantings of early bulbs are spectacularly successful. Drifts of snowdrops, *Narcissus pseudonarcissus* 'Princeps' (the Lent Lily), and *N. poeticus*, which flowers from April to June, do well here. *Crocus tommasinianus*, with its lovely slender flowers, can be relied on year after year, self-seeding generously.

Even before these, there are the winter aconites, *Eranthis hyemalis*, which can flower in time for Christmas. They are petulant and difficult to establish, but if they do settle your reward will be a large carpet of yellow which shows up well under a light fall of snow. Just talking about them has reminded me of how welcome they were in my last garden, cheerful even on the darkest days of winter around a sycamore that had sprung up in a disused drain.

In the wild, many bulbs and plants are designed to live under deciduous trees, where they have plenty of light and moisture from October to May, then heavy shade and dryness the rest of the time. In their undisturbed habitats, nature feeds them a perfectly balanced diet, but in the artificially controlled environment of a smaller garden this doesn't happen naturally. A nutritious top dressing of mulch in spring and autumn, plus the odd handful of bonemeal to encourage spent bulbs to grow again, is essential for good results. The tree will snaffle about four-fifths of this, and everything else will get the leftovers, so they need all the help they can get.

For ages the trees in my garden had me stumped. After the spring bulbs, which included hundreds of the Spanish bluebell and its white sister, there was nothing but desert for a yard all around the lime, which is most of the width of the garden. As summer advanced, the prospect from my sitting-room window grew more derelict, with a mess of decaying bluebell foliage as the main attraction. The only thing for it was to make a woodland garden around the tree, which I am slowly achieving through trial and error.

Working from the tree as centre, there are now hardy spring and autumn cyclamen planted right up to the trunk. Unfortunately, they are few because I stopped collecting them when I discovered that most of them are dug up in the wild. Instead I'll try seeds to increase my stock. The windflowers, *Anemone nemorosa* and *A. blanda*, have taken a grip. White foxgloves have started to flourish there and violas, both *odorata* and the purple-leaved *labradorica*, are flourishing.

A Mexican orange blossom, *Choisya ternata*, is finally growing properly and even gave sweet flowers last year, after I threatened it with the chop. A sage, some lavender and salvia are doing all right nearby. Variegated ground elder, which is decorous and spreads slowly and prettily, unlike the common stuff, is surviving here, making a good contrast with *Euphorbia robbiae*, itself a thug but controllable in such a small space. If cow parsley drifts in, it can look very decorative at the base of the tree for months.

Erythronium dens canis, the dog's tooth violet, which has lovely marbled foliage, is struggling bravely. *Polemonium,* the common blue and white Jacob's ladder, are thriving a bit farther out from the trees. The lovely thug rose, 'Belvedere', is in the very worst corner, hard up against next-door's big hedge where nothing else would grow. Only eighteen months old, it's already halfway up the lime, while the rest of its Herculean tentacles have to be chopped regularly or they leap out and make a grab for passersby. It'll have to go, before it pulls down the tree, but not just yet.

The lacy fern, *Polypodium vulgare 'Cambricans'*, likes dry shade and makes lovely foliage from August onwards. Bulbs that flower in summer, maybe the elusive little *Lapeirousia laxa,* will have to be found. Snakeshead fritillaries will go in, and maybe the daffodils could be followed by *Ornithogalum nutans,* which has strange, hyacinth-like greenish flowers, silvery within. There are colchicums, *Iris foetidissima, Arum italicum pictum,* hardy geraniums, brunnera … Not everything will work, but the only sure way to find out is to try.

Iris foetidissima

The Draughtsman's Garden

Everyone talks about painters and gardens. What about a draughts-man's approach? Charlie Cullen, though a painter and, more than that, head of painting at the National College of Art & Design, made his reputation as a brilliant draughtsman. His town garden close to the Grand Canal in Dublin is a testament to his drawing skills.

'It's a minimal garden,' he says. 'I wanted it to look dramatic and dense, with huge jungle foliage, a bit like a Rousseau painting, but I'd been neglecting it a bit and then this dog arrived last year and made holes everywhere. He's a very nice dog, but I've sort of given up on taking pride in the garden for the moment.'

He has no reason to be apologetic. The garden, twenty-five feet long and thirteen wide, down half a storey from street level at the back, looks like another country when you first see it partially framed by the open hall door. It is a draughtsman's dream, beautifully mapped out on four subtly rising levels, joined by straight cobbled paths and squared sets of steps. A fifth level, made by a series of rectangular raised beds, adds to the movement and extraordinary peace of this courtyard garden, each carefully delineated planting space making a self-contained drawing that lends itself easily to the broader picture.

If there was absolutely nothing planted here, this garden would stand on its own. Charles Cullen is quite pleased with what he calls its 'skeleton' and reckons he can easily resurrect it, though he joked that it looked like a rusty tin can in winter. Where the walls of old stone and peachy-yellow brick were not high enough for his 'country haven in the city', he added strong, squared trellis which holds *Clematis armandii* and *montana*, honeysuckle, passion flowers which fruit in one of the garden's many little microclimates, jasmines winter and summer, and variegated ivies in a hidden alcove used for potting and the clothesline.

The sky is largely excluded by the rustling canopy of a cherry tree standing dead centre, which hits you straight between the eyes when you look out through a glass wall at garden level. Alone and unpollinated since it lost its companion to honey fungus, the cherry, planted by the previous owner, hardly flowers and rarely fruits; cats use it to ambush birds, who've stopped coming, and it blocks three-quarters of the light.

He knows it will have to go when he 'gets back to the garden', but is reluctant to chop it down, talking instead of a drastic professional pruning. 'I love the effect it gives up so close, the sensation of being in a jungle or woodland. There is a great feeling of hope when you look at a tree first thing in the morning.' When he moved here over ten years ago, the neighbours had geese and a cock, dogs barked, birds chattered in the cherry tree, then but 'a lithe young thing', as he puts it. In almost shocking contrast to the city streets outside, the garden was, and still is, extraordinarily quiet, and the idea came to him that he could have an oasis in his adoptive town, a small part of the large garden he loved as a child growing up on Main Street, Longford.

On the way to his studio in Henrietta Street, he's noticed that the wild hart's tongue fern and even some mosses have been creeping back into the city. 'Mosses in particular are a good barometer of air pollution. I think the city has got much cleaner since we stopped burning bituminous fuel.' One of his raised beds contains native ferns under a wild hypericum.

A pink fuchsia and chinese lanterns grow a step down, gathered as cuttings and pods at Lissadell in County Sligo. A great stand of the tall native yellow flag iris waves about on a higher bed, having completely devoured a beloved stand of the even taller, cultivated blue. A step comfortable for sitting divides them from an equally large group of Arum lilies.

He shows me a slightly askew step which harbours water and encourages Baby's Tears, *Soleirolia*, to lap softly around the edges of the hard surfaces. A small collection of cacti sit on setts in the sunny corner, basking while he admires their shapes and thinks about making a cactus garden for them. Beautiful pieces of pottery by his late sister-in-law Maureen Hosty, whose work can be seen in the National Museum, are set against a dark wall. This brilliantly composed space, despite having no more than twenty different plant types, is one of the liveliest and most interesting gardens I've ever seen.

Reinventing a Small City Garden

'By the way,' a friend suddenly remarked last week, 'you wouldn't come over and look at my yard?' Now, I've often looked at this friend's yard, and while it's a perfectly good yard at the back of an artisan house in Stoneybatter, its air of hopeless abandonment usually defeated me. All he has is a little brick-built raised bed at the totally shaded end away from the house, and over the years a variety of people have made an effort and planted a bit of this and that in it. Occasionally their efforts have been rewarded with a daffodil, or two periwinkle leaves.

But now, disappointed by the barren, scentless scenery all around him as he drifts in his hammock, he wants an explosion of growth, a bloody jungle by early summer, a place to set his senses reeling until autumn. But, he says, it must look after itself. He really means this: this man would never get around to watering, so for a start, any container-growing would be strictly limited.

This leaves the deeply shaded, pathetically small and rather ugly L-shaped raised bed, measuring nine feet across the end, two feet long at the tail of the L, and just twenty-seven inches deep. The entire yard is twenty feet long by ten feet wide. A beautiful, weatherproof trestle table, made by joiner Brigitte de la Malene, measures three feet by six and dominates the centre. The floor is paved with ordinary, pinky-terracotta concrete slabs, but an artist friend has painted two of the walls a beautiful, faded terracotta with hints of orange and burnt yellows. The main house wall is mellow old yellow brick, the return wall white, and the pretty door and windows are painted the lovely dark blue of Mallorca.

My friend protested when I told him some of his concrete slabs would have to go, to make room for his jungle to grow, but he was persuaded that this wouldn't make his house fall down. There is no money for structural work, like a pergola, a wall fountain or even raising the height of the wall between him and the neighbours. But there is money for plants, plenty of John Innes No. 3 compost, sharp sand for drainage and natural soil conditioners and fertilizers.

On the sunniest wall, the main house wall facing south-west, the fast-growing *Solanum crispum* 'Glasnevin' will take pride of place. Almost evergreen in a sheltered inner-city space like this one, its royal blue flowers should cover much of the wall by summer and lend an exotic note. At the other side of the window, behind the kitchen door, I'll plant the golden hop (*Humulus aureus*), where it will clamber quickly up to his bedroom window, put him to sleep and grow over on down to decorate the sloping roof of the kitchen.

We're already into a shady area, so on the other side of the kitchen door I'm going for broke and planting the deliciously apple-scented, wildly enthusiastic and repeat-flowering creamy rose, 'Alberic Barbier', which can grow to nearly twenty feet and should meet and marry the golden hop up on the sloping roof. Along the ground-floor bathroom wall, past the two shores, we're getting into really heavy shade and here it's got to be a honeysuckle, one with yellows and pinks, heavily scented, that will flower for half the year and cover the wall quickly – either *Lonicera heckrottii* 'Gold Flame', or *L. periclymenum* 'Belgica', which is not so all-embracing but is very pretty.

Along the terracotta party wall more slabs will be lifted and a yellow rose, 'Lady Hillingdon', will go in. A red clematis, probably the informal, free-flowering 'Mme Jules Correvan', will soon intertwine with it. The little beds made by removing the slabs will be underplanted with *Viola cornuta* in the shade, sweet-scented clove carnations and stocks where it's brighter. Annual sweet pea could also go in here to lend extra colour and fragrance. I'll risk two pots, big ones, for *Lilium speciosum* and the wonderful red *Lobelia* 'Queen Victoria'.

Now on to the nasty bit at the back, the modern-brick bed. This doesn't make it to the wall on one side, leaving a dank corner of the yard which I've decided to fill with soil for growing ferns: maybe a big shuttlecock, or elegant *Onocleaya*, the Sensitive Fern, and some old-fashioned Lily of the Valley. There is already a thriving

Pyracantha, which should be trained against the wall, where it could act as a host for the Scottish flame flower, *Tropaeolum speciosum,* a scarlet climber to die for, which gives pure indigo berries after flowering.

An evergreen euonymus overhangs from a neighbour at the back and this will be cut back, the existing *Clematis montana* (*rubra,* I think) trained to flower all over it and the wonderfully accommodating rose, 'Mme Alfred Carrier', planted to do the same and more. The little bit of ground space is difficult for summer colour. So the perennial yellow foxglove, which tolerates shade, will go in, with *Hosta halcyon* (blue) in front. The colourful wood spurge, *Euphorbia amygdaloides* 'rubra' (*purpurea*) should do alright here, as will red kaffir lilies (for later), *Bergenia* 'Ballawley' *purpurascens, Viola labradorica,* more hostas, some pink Japanese anemones, some of the smaller spring bulbs and fragrant white summer jasmine.

I have a few other ideas, including lots of annuals; buddleia is sure to find its way in, butterflies, birds and bees ditto, and my friend can enter his hammock next summer secure in the belief that he swings in a fragrant jungle.

Lily of the Valley

Planting a Potager

In the winter it's tempting, as I look at the scruffy patches of bare earth increasing daily in my small back garden, to start planning a potager right outside the french windows in the kitchen. A sturdy and decorative vegetable and fruit garden, held in check by edible edging herbs, the centre filled with tall, beautiful and nourishing plants that will look good all winter, is a proposition worth considering.

Some snobbery still surrounds the placing of the kitchen garden, or potager. The fashion for informal cottage gardens, where food, roses and flowers are all grown willy-nilly together, is well established and socially acceptable. But the ordered kitchen garden still has associations with the bigger houses, with paid cooks and gardeners, with service. Maybe it's not the best view from the drawing or dining rooms, but most people prepare their own food nowadays and it is, for the cook and gardener, a deeply satisfying view from the kitchen.

Squares, triangles, rectangles, circles, a whole range of geometric shapes could greet you for breakfast. In my case, it would be just one of these shapes, with an established bay tree kept in pyramid form dominating. A shapely bay in a container would be the perfect focus point for a small, square potager and would not rob the soil of any goodness. For contrast in winter, it could be underplanted with white cyclamen.

Because this bit of garden will be centre-stage from the kitchen, use evergreen plants as edgings. These could be made of herbs, like the evergreen Winter Savory (*Satureja montana*), which has pretty white or mauve flowers well into early winter. It is good rubbed on insect bites, as an aid to digestion and as a disinfecting throat gargle; and its slightly coarse, peppery flavour is useful in winter cooking when thyme is scarce.

Another good edging herb is the evergreen golden oregano.

Origanum vulgare 'Compactum' would be a good one. It is gold-tipped, well-flavoured and small, though it seldom flowers and goes green as winter closes in. Like all the marjorams, it has some sedative properties and makes a soothing tea. As with the savory, it is good for picking all winter, for salads and stews. But don't neglect to have the tender *Origanum majorana*, or sweet marjoram, for summer cooking, with its stronger scent and finer flavour.

Parsley is another edible edging, though it does shrink considerably in winter and may not make bold enough lines. Chives look good as a summer edging, but because they die back and disappear completely in winter, they don't suit my case. Non-running strawberries are valuable in the small garden, but look a bit sad in winter. An alternative to herbs is to edge in box, but it would have to be kept neat, low and nourished, for it is a hungry feeder, robbing the soil all around it of nutrients. Decorative, frilly and multi-coloured, ornamental cabbages could also be a winter winner, if you like them, but you should grow from seed as buying enough plants for the purpose would be prohibitively expensive.

In the low light of winter, when colour takes on a different intensity, one of my favourite vegetables is the stately Buck Mulligan of the vegetable world, the purple-sprouting broccoli. Expensive and difficult to buy in season in Ireland, it should always be grown in home gardens so that its exquisite flavour when freshly picked may be appreciated. Even the spears or stalks, also known as Italian asparagus, are a welcome delicacy when little else is available. It crops for a long season, from late January to early May.

Red varieties of Brussels sprouts also give tall, outstanding winter colour, and flowering or ornamental curly kale makes edible posies of some brilliance. Tall, straight and great for sautéing and soup, leeks look well in winter contrast to any of these brassicas and if there are a few left flowering they add shape and interest. If you have room for an architectural statement, then the shapely rosemary, 'Miss Jessop's Upright', can be planted to emphasize each corner.

Obviously, all these can be underplanted with spring bulbs, though it might be difficult to keep from damaging them when putting in the next seasonal crops. The White Triumphator tulip could be sunk in pots and lifted when finished flowering, along with other gems of the bulb world. Preparation of the soil is vital for the hungry vegetables to come. Dig in plenty of compost or any organic mulching material you can lay hands on. The site should be level and you could incorporate a small, perhaps cobbled, area in the centre for your big pot or favourite garden ornament.

Evergreens

In winter, when the leaves have fallen from trees and shrubs and herbaceous foliage has gone to ground, a garden without some defining structure will collapse into chaos. Without strong bones to carry it through the lean months, it is an eyesore, giving little if any pleasure until the first bulbs break through again in spring.

This is a terrible waste. A garden should remain recognizable, a place of interest, comfort and retreat, all year round. Along with hard landscaping – walls, paths, pergolas, terracing, pools, paved yards, and a stream if you're lucky – evergreen plants provide the bone structure, the visible threads that run through a vibrant garden and link it all together into a successful whole within the wider landscape.

When all around them has changed utterly, evergreen plants remain, a constant element in the garden's architecture. Evergreens also act as a permanent buffer against noise pollution and as a screen between you and anything you don't want to see. Later in the year, when the broadleaved trees are finally bare, listen out for the difference in sound level. This is particularly relevant if you live *in urbis*.

September is the best month to plant evergreens. There is warm earth and time enough left for their roots to become established before the cold hits and everything slows down. An evergreen need not necessarily be green – it can be a variety of golds, silvers, reds and even glaucous blues. It's just a plant that looks largely the same all year, some shedding leaves as new ones grow. But it's always got leaves and it's always growing, never fully dormant.

Despite looking so solid and strong in winter, evergreen trees and shrubs are actually more tender than deciduous kinds. Susceptible to damage by frost, wind and too much sun, most of them are best planted where there's some shade and shelter from north and east winds. Some, such as the Mexican orange blossom *Choisya*, camellias and types of azaleas, rhododendrons, ceanothus and berberis, have flowers as well.

A clipped evergreen hedge looks wonderful at any time, but is particularly welcome in winter when it can stop a garden from falling apart completely. Yew (*Taxus*) has always been the fashion for top-notch hedges. Its status has grown further since the publication of *Yew and Non-U*, an amusing little book on gardening snobbery, and more so since yew clippings came into demand. Because they contain the active ingredient in Taxol, an anti-cancer drug, a collection scheme has been started in England.

The upright Irish yew, *Taxus baccatus* 'Fastigiata', makes an excellent columnar statement and lends great dignity to a smallish garden if planted at the end of a path or to define a corner. As a backdrop it is, in my view, unparalleled. But yew is not for everybody. Some find it too gloomy and dark, an uncomfortable reminder of sombre old graveyards. The image of death it carries is not helped by poets like Tennyson, who wrote:

> *Dark Yew, that graspest at the stones*
> *And dippest towards the dreamless head,*
> *To thee, too, comes the golden hour,*
> *When flower is feeling after flower.*

If yew scares you off but you still want an evergreen upright column or two as focal points, then there's the softer, fragrant, bluey-green upright Irish Juniper, *J. hibernica*. But I'm biased in favour of yew, particularly after falling in love a few years ago with a very particular private garden on the outskirts of Dublin city.

This garden is a formal square, enclosed within a much larger garden by high walls made entirely of darkest clipped yew. There are two portals cut cleanly at opposite sides. In the centre is a white-painted belvedere of sorts, made of wrought metal, with cool slates for seats. Each of the four corners is guarded by beautiful, larger than life, pale stone statues of men and women in classically romantic clothes. The only other plants in this deeply calming garden are some carefully spaced apple trees, very old and pollarded in the Continental way to make them short, strong and wide. I have been there in winter and summer, but have yet to see it in apple blossom time, when the pale flowers set against the dark yew must bring it close to an earthly paradise.

An exotic evergreen, not yet widely known and therefore a bit of a show-stopper, is the sea-green *Melianthus major*, the honey flower from South Africa which carries enormous, beautifully serrated leaves on curving stems with infinite poise, to a height of at least seven feet and the same or more across. Think carefully before you place it. Mine has grown alarmingly in its second year in the ground and should have been planted much farther back in the border or in a big pot. It's a rather tender, shrubby plant for milder and seaside districts and can be cut to the ground by a heavy frost. Last winter didn't seem to affect it at all. If frost does cut it down, it will re-sprout from the base the following year. My own fine specimen emits a not-quite-pleasant smell when the leaves are bruised or even brushed against – a smell of peanuts, according to some people. Personally speaking, if peanuts smelt like that I wouldn't eat them.

A bay tree is a beautiful thing and useful for the cooking pot. Though it can grow to thirty or more feet, it can be kept clipped to a size suitable for the smallest gardens. Remember, though, that very severe pruning leaves it vulnerable to attack by scale insects.

Hedgerows

The first quiet days of November, when the pomp and finery of autumn has fallen to earth, are the best time to appreciate the glories of a well-laid hedgerow. After a flush of spring interest, the hedgerows retreat into the summer background, going largely unnoticed until late autumn and early winter. It is when all is bare around them that they again come into their own. An abundance of hips, haws, fruits nuts and berries light up the short, drizzly days. So too does the prospect of sloe gin for Christmas, accompanied by ripened hazelnuts. Or mulled elderberry wine, or cherry plum sauce, all part of the eating and drinking to be found in a good hedgerow.

If you are thinking of planting a hedge, as a screen or a barrier to people and animals, you could consider making your own productive hedgerow of sorts. It takes a farmer, an expert, to lay a perfectly balanced one, but there's no reason you should let that keep you from the powerful kick of your own sloe gin.

Your hedgerow could be made up of blackthorn, for its wealth of white blossom in spring, its dark purple sloes, and its thorny tips, which are ideal proof against intruding humans or animals. Blackthorn (*Prunus spinosa*) is a very hardy member of the plum family which will stand hacking back into shape whenever necessary. Eventually, if left to itself, it makes a fat, shrubby tree rarely more than twelve feet in height.

The next component of the eating and drinking hedge could be elder. Besides feeding the birds, the berries make a wine that passes muster at parties when mulled. The wide, creamy flowerheads in June make a *Champagne methodoise* in six weeks, which I'm told is volatile stuff with a dodgy cellar life, often exploding from its bottle with a terrible bang before you open it. It takes six weeks to mature and is a light enough drink.

The wild elder, *Sambucus nigra*, is perfect for coppicing and the cheapest to buy, or you can take cuttings very easily from an established one. Just take twelve-to-fifteen-inch cuttings of hardwood and stick them into a narrow slit in the soil lined with grit. They'll be ready for transplanting to your hedge by the same time next year. Elder grows to about the same height as the blackthorn but much faster, with new shoots making up to five feet in a season. Cutting out a third of the oldest growth every year should keep them within bounds.

The cherry plum, *Prunus cerasifera*, has fruits about double the size of sloes that make stony but tasty pies, jams or a rich liqueur. Along with damsons, it could be another candidate for your hedge. Both, of course, have the usual delicate spring blossom of their tribe. *Rugosa* roses, with their long season of flower followed by big red or orange hips bursting with vitamin C, are another possible inclusion.

Apples, perhaps a crab, and cultivated blackberries can all join in the party along the way, the blackberries when the hedge has grown to about four feet. Plant them at intervals along the hedge, tying in shoots where necessary. Cultivated blackberries are much bigger and have fewer pips than the wild ones, and should be treated like raspberries by removing completely their fruited canes and tying in the new growth.

Recently, a friend made the point that a whole generation of children has now grown up without ever having seen the common elm (*Ulmus procera*), which has been virtually wiped out by Dutch elm disease, so-called because the scientists who first researched it were Dutch. Research into disease-resistant strains is looking good and with luck the lovely English Elm could make a comeback. Widely planted in the eighteenth century as a hedgerow timber tree, there's no eating or drinking on the elm, but if you'd like to include it then perhaps the disease-resistant Siberian Elm (*Ulmus pumila*) would be more suitable. A small, fast-growing, leafy, almost evergreen tree with a flat domed head, it would be a good winter hedge-thickener.

Anyone who enjoys hacking things back will love having the handsome native hazels. They thrive on this kind of treatment, living to be a hundred years old and more. The coppiced wood, which was widely used in thatching, makes perfect, branched pea sticks. Though hazels are mostly self-fertile with both female and male plants carrying yellow catkins, planting different kinds together can improve yields. A properly pruned bush will take five to six years to start cropping heavily, when it will give about twenty pounds of cobs in mid-autumn. These can be left to dry on the floor of a shed or in the sun for a couple of weeks, then stored in a dry place where they should keep well until spring. Feed your hedge well, and yourself on the nuts, washed down with a deeply satisfying slug of sloe gin which, be warned, can take the legs from under you.

Edging Herbs

In the wildest part of my garden, the various self-sown feverfews, *Tanacetum parthenium*, proved themselves staunch allies against a recent onslaught of wind and heavy rain. Not only did this under-valued member of the chrysanthemum family remain standing to attention when others were cowering on the ground, but where it had been ordered to do border patrol as a lowish hedge along the further reaches of the path it made an extraordinarily effective support for the big geraniums, particularly the loose-living deep blue *grandiflorum* under the Bramley, firmly keeping it from falling over the edge.

I will definitely use it again to contain some of the great perennial border sprawlers, as it is so much prettier than stakes and metal supports. Feverfew is a pungently aromatic annual to perennial herb, most probably native to south-eastern Europe but now found as a garden escapee here, in the rest of Europe and in the Americas. It has daisy-like flowers which appear from May to October, reaches about twenty-four inches in height and comes in a decorative golden form, *aureum*, and a double, 'Flore Pleno'. It can be bought as a plant or sown from seed and will thrive and seed freely almost anywhere.

As its common name suggests, it has been used for reducing fevers for centuries, also as a nerve tonic, for headaches and for curing arthritis. Its relatives the tansys (used in black puddings and as a spring tonic in the west of Ireland) and *Tanacetum cinerariifolium* are powerful insecticides and were used to worm children, delouse dogs and cats and preserve the dead from putrefaction. Growing it around drains and outside the kitchen door helps disinfect and keep flies at bay.

After much modern research feverfew is now formally acknowledged as a source of great relief to some migraine sufferers. It is sometimes available in capsule form, or try a leaf or two in a salad or between slices of bread and butter. Eaten on its own it's very bitter and in some very sensitive individuals it may cause a slight skin rash or nasty little mouth ulcers. Because it is also known to regulate menstrual cycles, it should never, ever be taken in any form by pregnant women.

Using herbs as hedges alongside paths or as containment for a more formal, geometric gathering of flowers and vegetables is as useful and practical as it is pretty. I love the traditional box edging, but it can be expensive to set up in any decent amount, taking up quite a lot of room in a small garden and more than its fair share of nourishment from the soil. It also requires two decent haircuts a year and the trimmings, while sometimes good for striking cuttings, usually end up on the compost heap. On the plus side, it is neat, evergreen and in winter has a good skeleton, particularly under snow.

Long-lived evergreen herbs that can be used as edging include lavender, hyssop and low-growing germander. Pruning them also means reaping a harvest of flowers and foliage with a variety of culinary, cosmetic and medicinal uses. No linen drawers or presses can have enough lavender. For small gardens, however, the standard English lavender's sense of large-scale drama might not be practical. Recently, I was given a packet of a dwarf variety to sow, which is billed as ideal for hedging and reaches only eighteen inches. So far, 'Cambridge Lady' has produced twenty-nine seedlings, but as I haven't seen it properly yet, I can't vouch for it. If the packet's claims are true, then spaced twelve inches apart these should give one roughly twenty-eight feet of perfectly behaved edging to play around with.

Lavender is easy to grow from seed or autumn cuttings. It likes a well-drained place and a fair amount of sun. Its flowers should be harvested before they are quite fully open, and dried quickly. After flowering, an overall trim will keep it in shape and stop it becoming too leggy. It resents having any of its old wood cut, so it pays to groom it when young.

'Purge me with Hyssop and I shall be clean' sings the Bible of this herb, once used for cleansing holy places. Hyssop is lovely, a bushy hardy perennial native to southern Europe and eastern Asia. It can reach thirty-six inches, though twenty-four is more usual. Rock Hyssop, 'Aristatus', is similar but smaller and more compact, with blue flowers in August.

Hyssop's flowers are rich blue, white or pink depending on variety and arrive in middle to late summer. Its leaves are narrow and aromatic and it needs to be trimmed in late spring to keep it compact. It is notoriously slow to germinate from seed. I remember sowing it hopefully years ago in another garden and eventually getting a paltry three plants, of which one survived.

If you want a larger number, you'd probably be better off buying a few well-grown nursery plants and dividing the roots or taking cuttings in spring and autumn. Minute quantities of the bitter leaves are used in salads and strong soups and as a digestive in fatty foods, and the oil of hyssop flowers is used to flavour liqueurs, notably Chartreuse. Both leaves and flowers infused as a *tisane* have an antiseptic and cleansing effect on sore throats. Grow it in a light soil in some sun and watch the bees homing in on it. Hyssop honey is delicious.

Germander, *Teucrium x lucidrys*, used as an edging, is something I only came across recently in an article by Anna Pavord, which was accompanied by a fetching photograph of it outlining a formal herb garden. It looks very relaxed and could easily replace box in a knot garden. Eventually reaching about sixteen to eighteen inches, it has minute, scented, lobed leaves and good pink flowers which go on for months. A light clip in either spring or autumn is all that's needed to keep it in shape. Used extensively in the making of alcoholic drinks, it grows well from seed or cuttings and enjoys life in the sun, out of the wind's way.

Colour

Fashions in colour come and go but good taste never needs to change. You know it when you see it and its rightness bestows a kind of peace, like a benediction. Argue all you like about what constitutes good taste; one look at the bedlam created by the colour combinations in many spring gardens will leave you in no doubt about the definition of bad taste.

Yellows and pinks together are the biggest screamers in the early spring gardens around my way. The trouble really starts with the leathery Elephants' Ears, the *Bergenias*, whose early pink flowers clash straightaway with the yellow of crocus, winter aconites, jasmine, the first non-white daffodils and any early yellow wallflowers. Then we move on, say, to the unnerving yellows of most Forsythia, which shoot up and dominate every horizon, then immediately do battle with the huge clan of pink flowering cherries which bloom at the same time.

Playing with colour is one of gardening's greatest pleasures, but in a small garden in particular you have to be really disciplined because there's not a lot of space to screen off incompatible colours. A good way to study colour is to look at abstract painting, where the relationship between colours is so vital.

Gillian Ayers, an English abstract artist whose paintings sell for many thousands of pounds, manages to combine bright yellows and pinks triumphantly. I wish this were as easy to achieve in the garden. I've made a few experimental yellow and pink combinations, but with shockingly bad results. Monet, fashionable amongst gardeners at the moment, is easier to follow. He made a garden to paint, and changed it all the time to suit whatever new picture came into his mind.

If you've been feeling uneasy about some of the colour schemes that greeted you in your plot this spring, you can take up your artist's palette during the winter and play Great Painters, while noticing that colour changes with the light at different times of day. Pick a bunch of the different flowers you want to move and stick them into the ground here and there until you find the perfect spot, taking into account their foliage, texture, height and form in relation to their new planting partners.

The same patch of ground can easily accommodate a change of colour scheme later in the season with careful planning. When all the early pinks have gone, you can allow some yellows in with all the others, and the leaves of the louder pinks remain to make ground cover, one of the great secrets of good gardening. Even blues can be a problem in the spring garden, where the true blue of a brunnera will completely cancel out the delicate lavender-blue of an *Anemone nemorosa*.

Mauve, meaning 'bright and delicate' according to the dictionary, used to be an acceptable word but for years has been out of fashion. 'Women', wrote the late garden writer Beverley Nichols, 'seem to have come to the conclusion that mauve does something unkind to their complexions. I trust they will not allow this prejudice to extend to the garden.' The fey Mr Nichols, writing in the 1930s, is one of the few writers to put in a good word for poor old mauve, which has been described as a colour too blue to be pink, too pink for blue and not dark enough to be purple. It might be too subtle to fit into a Gertrude Jekyll border.

The classic Jekyll colour plan for the mixed border is safe to play around with and difficult to get completely wrong. From left to right, it goes along in the following order: greys and glaucous foliage / pure blues / grey blues / whites / pale yellows (including grasses) / absolutely palest pinks / oranges / and, at the centre, the reds in all their brilliance. Then you continue on, back down the scale again, except that on the way back down you put all the purples together after the pale yellows, because blue draws the eye down along too quickly whereas purples arrest you, and are difficult to place separately anyway. That's it, except that you may still be left holding a poor mauveish outcast, wandering around the garden forever trying to fit it in.

Green Gardening

It is the 7th of January as I write. By midnight yesterday the Christmas tree, stripped of its baubles, had to be taken down. Ditto with the holly and mistletoe. The house looks bare without them; because they were only installed on Christmas Eve, they didn't have a chance to outlive their welcome. The question of how best to recycle the discarded festive greenery was made more urgent somehow by reading a scary article in *The Irish Times* on the consequences for Ireland of global warming.

What's the connection, you might well ask. A few humble bits of greenery dumped by a million households on one island is not going to make any difference to the greenhouse effect, is it? Christmas trees are grown as a consumer crop like any other, so if your area has a recycling collection you can easily be rid of the sad skeleton and the guilt that goes with it. Or, as we do, use bits of the oil-laden branches in the fire for a bit of a spark. The trunk makes a sturdy and useful garden pole till it rots, or you can cut it into small logs for drying and burning.

Shrivelled holly, prickly and not easily composted, makes a volatile ingredient in mixed kindling. Mistletoe, if it's native and you know what kind of tree it came from, can be propagated to secure the future of the kiss, at least. Make a slit high up in the bark of said tree (often old apples and pears) and squash in the berries, mixed with a bit of muck or mud. You might get lucky. If you do all or even some of these things, perhaps that will salve your conscience and establish you as an environmentally serious gardener, if only in your own mind.

Once the green bug bites a gardener, it's only a short step to a deep suspicion of toxic, noxious chemicals, be they weed-killers, fertilizers, sprays or slug pellets. We've come a long way from the time when every form of poison known to man was used indiscriminately by gardeners obedient to official edicts. Still alive in folk memory is the famous one on the efficacy and harmlessness of DDT, a chlorinated hydrocarbon pesticide, now completely discredited.

The growing wave of green consciousness has been reflected in the mostly organic advice now given by contemporary garden writers. If you look back even a few years, it's quite shocking how casually the gardening press recommended toxic remedies for insignificant garden ills. Even so, except for those writers who risk ridicule by the wearing of an uncompromising green, they are all agreed on the political correctness of using glyphosate-based weedkillers, which are only supposed to kill selected green tissues, working their way from leaf down to root. Then, it is claimed, the herbicide becomes neutral and harmless in the soil.

Other herbicides have been discredited in the past. Who's to say glyphosate won't fall foul at some time? Why, if they're so harmless, must they never be used near food crops? What happens to the residue when it rains? What insect life does it affect? I don't know yet, but as long as I have a small garden I'm not tempted to use it. I'll stick to the hoe and my wonderful French tool, 'the dandelion killer'.

There is no excuse for using toxic sprays and artificial fertilizers in any quantity. If you spray roses for mildew, blackspot and aphids they all come back again, eventually. If you use slug pellets there's always the risk of killing birds and making your cats and dogs sick. Much more enjoyable to slice them in half with the dandelion killer, though their friends and family make a gruesome sight eating their remains, as they are wont to do. Alas, I've gone soft on snails. It's the way they might look at you, their eyes held sweetly erect on stalks. I can only bear to throw them over the wall into the back lane, to forage elsewhere.

Helpful Insects

Slugs, flea beetles, vine weevils and aphids are among the gardener's worst enemies and should be murdered on sight by trapping, squashing, stamping or slicing them in half. But chemical controls should never be used. Besides fouling up the atmosphere and leaving residues in the soil to be washed into streams and rivers, they annihilate the good guys.

The good guys among the insects are not pests at all. Some of them are harmless and even more are positively beneficial, allies in the fight against the bad guys. Some pollinate plants, including fruit trees, and without them there would be no crops. Others attack and kill and still others are parasites on other insects, which helps keep down the enemy populations.

Everybody knows the ladybird beetle, usually red or orange, but there are over forty different kinds and all except one rare one, which has twenty-four spots, prey on other harmful insects. Not so well known are the rather unfortunate looking, quick-moving ladybird larvae, often slate-blue in colour with orange or yellow spots. The larvae are even more valuable than the adult, gobbling up three hundred aphids apiece while still in their infancy. Depending on type, ladybirds will also eat scale insects (hard-pruned bay trees in pots are prone to these), mealybugs, thrips and red spider mites. Lacewings, which sometimes come indoors to hibernate, are small and beautiful, with pale green, delicately veined wings. Their larvae are unprepossessing, resembling an oval caterpillar studded with tufts of hair. But like its parent, it feasts on pests.

The long-legged black beetle that scuttles away when you lift up stones or debris in the garden is the Carabid or ground beetle and should never be hurt. It and its larvae feed on cabbage-root maggots amongst other things. The decline of the glow-worm is to be mourned, not just because so few people here will ever see these lovely creatures lighting up the night, but also because their young eat slugs and snails. A colony of them would be a boon in any garden.

It pays too to encourage the elegant damsel and dragonflies, which hover and dart about in summer, particularly near water. The lovely creatures are incapable of stinging or biting a human, but they are a menace to harmful pests. Hoverflies, like slender wasps that can remain suspended for ages and then suddenly dart to their prey, are ace eaters of aphids, gobbling over a hundred each per hour. They have no sting and are perfectly safe.

Capsid bugs are not all enemies, though some of them do nibble on leaves while others feed on adult insects and their eggs. The word parasite is usually used pejoratively, but not in the case of the amusing-looking little Ichneumon flies. *Apanteles glomeratus*, to use its scientific name, is a real friend, laying its eggs inside the caterpillars of the horribly destructive Large Cabbage White Butterfly which, as a result, never gets to grow up. Sorry about that.

Coping with Frost

Frost always comes suddenly and takes us by surprise. By then it is often too late to save the most vulnerable plants. Maybe all gardeners should adopt the old scouting motto 'Be Prepared', and pin it somewhere they're bound to pass every day. Plants growing in pots, tubs, raised troughs and sinks are most at risk. Their survival depends on human intervention. Which means you, the gardener, the person who imprisoned them there for your own enjoyment in the first place.

For the gardener with a clear conscience, just being there in the winter garden, when it is spellbound by ice and the hurly-burly of work and nature has suddenly been stilled, can be deeply pleasant. At those times too, there comes a sense of relief that the carousel of the seasons has halted for a while: that you are obliged to do nothing at all except check the greenhouse, read all the seed catalogues and feed and water the birds. Blue tits are especially welcome in the winter garden. They may knock the foil tops from the milk bottles and drink the cream, but they also eat greenfly, a major part of their winter diet.

If tender things are dying all around you, it will make you feel terrible, to the point where you find yourself avoiding the garden altogether for the winter. Which would be a shame, because you get to know its character very well when you can see its bare bones, or missing teeth. But there is nothing you can do when the ground is frozen solid, except think and dream as you stroll around admiring the shape of things under your domain, or indeed lamenting them.

Certainly digging when the ground is frozen is so bad for the structure of the soil that it shouldn't even be considered, unless you're digging foundations for walls, paths and other hard-landscaping jobs, which are best tackled in the winter when there is little growth and most foliage plants have retreated underground.

This year, most of the country has escaped any cruel frosts, which can sometimes hit us here around the second week of November. The weather has been so mild that the exotic, half-hardy Cape Honey Flower, *Melianthus major*, has soared to a staggering twelve feet in this garden (the books predict a maximum of eight) and in the last few weeks has produced an attractive, chocolate-red flowerhead rising from a stout, thirty-inch stem held aloft at the very top of the plant.

There is still time for those of you with a *laissez-faire* attitude to change your ways, to use this respite to protect your plants from the real possibility of lethal frostbite later on. With very little effort, a winter of discontent can be neatly avoided.

Plants in containers are at a disadvantage straightaway. Their straitjacketed roots are pathetically easy game. With only a shallow depth of soil and the walls of their containers between them and the icy, probing fingers of a killer frost, they have nowhere to hide should things get tough. Even perfectly hardy shrubs and plants that would normally hack a winter in the open ground are in danger, because we have chosen to grow them as captives in containers. The least we can do is look after them, wrap the hardier ones round with a blanket of fleece, bubble-wrap, straw, bracken or hessian of any kind – or plunge them, pot and all, into a pit filled with ashes from the fire. Mulch them with leaves, compost, bracken or even the last grass clippings, and where they're not too heavy, drag them into a sheltered spot in the garden or yard to wait out the winter. Potted lemon and orange trees will not, of course, stand a winter outside and should be lugged inside.

Some fuchsias, pelargoniums, begonias and other tender speci-mens should also be indoors by November. In fact, by bringing them into the house they can be encouraged to go on flowering for ages. If that's not an option, give them as much insulation and shelter as you can dream up, though I wouldn't bet on the begonias' survival.

Troughs or sinks for growing delectable, miniature alpines are par-ticularly at risk in very cold weather. Yes, of course, alpines are very hardy things. They come from mountain homes where the tempera-ture dips much lower than ours and snow covers them much of the time. But in their high or low alpine habitats, they can stretch their roots down deep between the rock crevices and find a safe berth in the perfect soil of their homeland. Planted in troughs, a rough approximation of their free-draining natural habitats is all that can be achieved by even the most dedicated alpine enthusiast. By definition, the depth of soil in a container will be too shallow to withstand very low temperatures. Certainly, anything as low as those recorded on the night of the 1st of January 1996, minus 21 or 22 I think, would have turned the few inches of soil in a raised alpine sink into a solid block of ice, which would squeeze the life out of a little plant or bulb left unprotected in its *faux* alpine habitat.

The same treatment as that mentioned for other containers will suit alpine troughs as well. Tie the wrappings on with strong twine. On particularly cold evenings, when you think you can sniff a frost coming your way, cover the top soil in the containers with something light, like the ubiquitous bracken, which can easily be removed when the air is warmer. If you leave it on, the plants will be deprived of air and rain and that won't do them much good either.

Garden Garb

'What do you wear when you're gardening?' an elegant woman wanted to know. Good question. Dressing for the garden is a serious business. If you don't take care, you end up with vicious scratches and splinters, infected cuts, hands and nails ingrained with dirt, chilblains, hair like straw dotted with twigs and leaves, chronic arthritis and a ruined complexion.

Novices often pose in picturesque outfits as their flirtation with gardening begins. For the women, perhaps strappy sandals and an ankle-length flowery dress that keeps tripping you up and snagging on everything. For the men, maybe expensive cords in earth colours, collarless linen shirts and hand-woven wool weskits. But after ruining the new Barbours, bibs and tuckers, having your arms mauled by a rose bush and catching a severe cold on a pet day in treacherous March, you learn.

That's not to say you can't look elegant in the garden. Nancy Lancaster, a founder of Colefax and Fowler and a noted gardener, looked amazingly so by all accounts – hair shortish, smart, well cut to stop it getting in her eyes as she worked, pruning her roses with her arms and hands protected by leather gauntlets. Her jackets were old and well worn, but obviously couture and made for her, so she could move freely. They were sturdy jackets, figured in at the waist, with beautiful cuffs and buttons – the height of utilitarian chic.

In every photograph of Vita Sackville-West taken in her garden at Sissinghurst, she is shod in incredibly long, handmade, lace-up leather boots over jodhpurs. Tying the laces must have been a nightmare, but they look impermeable and stunningly comfortable. Hair in a bob, well-shaped old cardigan over a pretty silk blouse and fag always in hand, she was a tall, striking equine figure as she prowled the castle grounds.

Garden Garb

I have never seen Helen Dillon without her pearls, their pale, shimmering beauty adding elegance to whatever she's wearing, whether it's mud-spattered blue plastic rain gear or a cool cotton jumper over rolled-up trousers. The late lamented novelist and gardener Molly Keane is reputed to have worn a toque, which would certainly have kept the Wurzel Gummidge hair look at bay. As for myself, the days of wearing my favourite old Richard Lewis crêpe skirts, cut flatteringly on the bias, teamed with a figured twill jacket, have long since gone.

Nowadays my clobber has got to be warm, and water- and thorn-proof. Denim jeans are good, with a pair of leggings worn underneath in winter. Comfortable warm boots with ankle protection stop you chopping off your foot or twisting your ankle. Buy a cheap waxed jacket (because they get ruined), or army and police surplus gear, which is tough and cheap and includes great trousers with useful tool pockets. Underneath I wear woolly vests and bloomers, i.e. knickers with legs that keep your thighs warm. They have a certain Edwardian charm.

I've given up on my hands, except when I have social obligations and remember to fill my nails with soap before mucking about, which makes them much easier to scrub clean. But they do feel like coarse-grade sandpaper, I must admit, and snag my good stockings. If there is hot sun, I sometimes rub almond oil in the *gruaig* to stop it drying out. And I never, ever go out in the elements without moisturizer, mascara, eye-cream and a necklace.

Plans and Records

Bare January is not the best time to dream up great planting ideas, unless you know where every dormant perennial and bulb is buried and remember how much space it occupied at the height of its season. But winter is definitely the best time to study the lines of a garden from every vantage point and decide what architectural work, green or otherwise, needs to be done to improve its structure.

The reason so many people fail to keep their New Year resolutions is because they make difficult and unpleasant ones. This is a mistake. Some gardening resolutions can be difficult and unpleasant too, like chopping down a fine tree growing in the wrong place, or banishing forever a pretty invader with imperial ambitions. But most are about improving the garden and, by extension, the quality of life, so they are no hardship.

Keeping a record of your gardening is one of the best resolutions a gardener can make. Records are incredibly useful for planning ahead, and old notes and design ideas make fascinating, often deeply informative, reading. Well, mine do, to paraphrase Oscar Wilde, who said he wouldn't be parted from his own diary because 'One should always have something sensational to read on the train.' Recently, I looked back on some planting notes made for the dry front garden while it was peaking in early summer, which I'm afraid it still does. These notes, if I may say so, were really good and clear, with plants carefully chosen so that the garden would continue to please throughout summer, autumn and winter.

All the work I put into the planning would have been forgotten, wasted, lost forever, if it weren't for those detailed notes and a rough little drawing showing the whereabouts of existing plants. Without them, I would have to think and measure it out all over again. Instead, I now have a fine blueprint to consult when the time comes for action.

To understand your garden better, first take photographs of it, in all seasons, from every window and door in the house and from every angle outside. With one of the new APS cameras, it's an easy, cheap, enjoyable way to get an overall picture of what's right and what's wrong, even if the snaps show up some truly shocking views. Then, in a special and spacious garden notebook, jot down your observations and ideas, using the photos as a reference. Should you change your mind later, having learnt something new about plants or design in the meantime, the original notes will still contain useful information and perhaps brilliant, off-the-cuff ideas which might never strike you again.

For making notes outdoors, a pocket-sized notebook with waterproof covers (made by Weatherall) is another essential piece of kit. Add to that a well-sharpened, reliable HB or B pencil of a good make, such as Faber Castell or Derwent Graphic. Pencils write in the rain; biros do not, and ink smears. Jot down plant names and colour combinations, sketching leaf shapes and design ideas as they occur to you in your own or other people's gardens. Later, you can transfer any relevant information to the mother notebook at your leisure, secure in the knowledge that some kind of record has been kept.

If you don't mind drawing on them (use felt-tip pens), photographs can be very useful guides, making it easy to see what is wrong. They allow you to play around with new, bolder shapes by superimposing them on the pictures. When you think you've got the situation sussed, it's time to see if your ideas will work in reality.

The best way to find out is to make an accurately scaled drawing of your site. Don't be daunted. Your drawing doesn't have to meet any professional standards, but it should be reasonably accurate and as easy to read as a map, which is what it is, really. Start by measuring out the space with a proper measuring tape.

Drawing to scale is not some impenetrable technical mystery. It just calls for a clear head and a basic grasp of simple arithmetic. Whether using the metric or the imperial system, the principle is the same. Take it that the chosen site measures thirty metres in length by fifteen metres in width. A piece of paper that size might fit into a grand ballroom, but not many people keep ballrooms these days. So you scale it down in proportion.

A scale of 1:100 is simplest to use: ten millimetres on paper represents one metre in the real world. Use a ruler and try to keep your lines straight and true. You will get better at this with practice and graph paper or a set square to guide you. When you've drawn the basic shape of the site, plus any hard landscaping features you want to retain, get copies of it made. Then continue by drawing in all the other existing features, once again to scale if you can manage it. If a site slopes, then measure the difference in height between the lowest and highest points. Relief lines might be called for if the slope is steep.

Remember also to note the direction of the sun, so that you don't get carried away and choose the wrong plants for the wrong place. Note too the extent of tree and shrub canopies, which cast shade, as do walls and buildings. When you've done that, you've got a drawing of the garden as it stands. Make copies of this too. Then you have numerous drawings of your garden to play around with.

A simple map or ground plan like this can be a revelation, giving you a bird's-eye view of the garden and bringing a new intimacy to your knowledge of it and its possibilities. There are, of course, much greater drawing skills employed by garden architects and designers, which bring a startling clarity and an almost tangible sense of three-dimensional space to their plans. But acquiring those skills involves years of study and practice and that, dear reader, is a another matter altogether.

PLANT PROFILES

Daffodils

Flower of the hour in early spring has to be the daffodil, beautiful in all but its blowsiest, over-bred forms, those vigorous cultivars the colour and texture of dead white flesh. There is widespread confusion about the difference between a daffodil and a narcissus – many people think that the big, trumpet-flowered fellas are the daffodils and the smaller, prettier ones with the flat, open faces and back-swept wings are the narcissi. In fact, botanically, they are one and the same thing.

Known variously as Daffys, Lenten Lilies, Lusa Crom Cinn, Daffydowndillys and Easter Lilies, they are so familiar and grow so happily here that most people, understandably, take them for an Irish native. Not so, though there are many singularly Irish forms of the cultivated daffodil which seem to have existed for a very long time.

Twenty-one species peculiar to Ireland were noted by the botanist F.W. Burbidge in 1889. He believed that our cool, moist climate led to seedling variations appearing more readily here than in English gardens, variations unknown as wild plants even in the parts of the Iberian Peninsula where the flora has links with Ireland and where the narcissus originated. Many of those listed by Burbidge were collected in old Irish gardens by Fanny Currey of Lismore in Co. Waterford, and by William Baylor Hartland, an early Cork-based nurseryman and dedicated collector of daffodils, tulips and apples. Ireland was especially rich in those delicate white trumpet daffodils of the *Narcissus moschatus, N. lpestris* and *N. albicans* groups.

Their names, according to Keith Lamb and Patrick Bowe in their excellent *History of Gardening in Ireland,* evoke nostalgia now: Minnie Warren, Robert Boyle, Countess of Desmond, Little Nell, Colleen Bawn and Bishop Mann were some of the old kinds that flourished when growing semi-naturalized in mossy, grassy places 'rather than in the highly cultivated ground demanded by the vigorous cultivars of today'.

Hartland collected with such enthusiasm that by 1883 he was able to compile his first daffodil catalogue, listing more than a hundred varieties. By 1886 his third catalogue contained more than 150 species. Nowadays, the Royal Horticultural Society of Britain has classified 20,000 or so daffodil cultivars in a dozen divisions, which has made identification much simpler.

If you thought that daffodils were yellow, or white and yellow, then last year's display at the Chelsea Flower Show would have surprised you. There were clear oranges, pinks and even reds. I didn't like them at all, though these colours are nothing new. Another Irish daffodil fancier, Guy Wilson, bred many seedlings in the early part of this century, including reds and pinks with names like Armada, Home Fires, Irish Rose and Passionale.

There's a huge amount of snobbery surrounding the humble daffodil, a member of the amaryllis or lily family, and it's true that some of the rubbery ones are a bit naff, having had all refinement and scent bred out of them. These big boors are also the ones which last forever, whose great strapping leaves refuse to die back and stare at you for months on end. The problem is that if you cut off their foliage after deadheading, the bulb won't get the nourishment it needs to flower well next year.

If you do have the larger types – and some of them are perfectly acceptable – then plant them near the back of a border where their dying leaves will soon be disguised by taller and later herbaceous perennials. The leaves of the prettier, smaller types are less obtrusive and die back quickly, without too much fuss, like those of the crocus and snowdrop.

Daffodils are amenable to being moved after flowering, though you often have to dig deep to get the bulbs out, especially if they are well established. It's best to move them while you can still see them, and picture their shape and colour in your mind's eye. If you wait until later you will invariably slice a good proportion of the bulbs with your spade, even if you've marked the spot.

Plant them in natural-seeming drifts – indeed, where they are naturalized in the wild, they seem to grow in bunches – but never in straight lines or regimented groups. And please don't tie their leaves into unsightly bunches with string, or bend them over to hide them, which stops half the nourishment getting back to the bulb.

With your trowel, dig an individual hole for each one, twice the depth of the bulb. Add a (gloved) handful of bonemeal if you still use it – I do in the front garden, where there are no herbs, fruit or veg. Fill the hole with water, drop the bulb in and backfill with the soil you removed, refreshed if necessary with a bit of compost. Mark the position clearly so you don't dig there by mistake later on in the season.

Places to see daffodils naturalized in 'hosts', as in Wordsworth's 'host of golden daffodils', are rare in the wild in Ireland, though the place the poet commemorated, the banks of the Ullswater in the English Lake District, still has an impressive 'wild' colony if you're passing that way.

Among the Irish places to see them 'fluttering and dancing in the breeze' are: Mount Usher in Ashford, Co. Wicklow; Florence Court in Enniskillen; Coolcarrigan near Naas in Kildare, open from April by appointment (phone 045 863512/863524); Helen Dillon's garden at 45 Sandford Road, Ranelagh, for the smaller, prettier narcissi; and the Guy Wilson Daffodil Garden at the University of Ulster, Coleraine.

Violas

The fanciful Elizabethan herbalist John Gerard wrote that the beauty and grace of the sweet-scented violets 'doth admonish and stir up a man to that which is comely and honest; for these flowers through their beauty, variety of colour and exquisite form do bring to a liberal and gentle manly mind the remembrance of honesty, comeliness and all kinds of virtues: for it would be an unseemly and filthy thing for him that doth look upon and handle fair and beautiful things, to have his mind not fair, but filthy and deformed'.

Sweet violets, violas, violettas, heart's ease and pansies are all members of the same fair and generous family, the *Violaceae*. They add an enormous amount to the garden virtually all year round. During mild winter spells and early in spring, their sweet, modest faces are particularly welcome. No sooner has one lot stopped flowering than another rushes to take its place.

In late autumn it's the turn of *Viola labradorica*, a choicer version of the wild violet, with sombre, purplish heart-shaped leaves, tiny flowers the colour of wine (well, meths really) and a bare, cool scent. At the moment there's a single spray of it in a tiny jar of water on my table, the first of winter. Its dark form is showing up very well against the old white and green china, which suggests it needs something lighter than itself to contrast with out in the garden.

V. labradorica has a reputation for running wild, seeding itself in places where it's not wanted and getting itself tangled around the roots of other plants. It does indeed do all of those things, but quite often its own choice of habitat is inspired, far more fetching than any we could have devised. If it has to be moved, it settles its thin roots down readily wherever you put it, even in the most unpromising places. The dark foliage is good all year round and looks well near granite and as a foil for small, pale bulbs. From December until the end of spring it will give flowers, sporadically at first but increasingly as the days get longer. No garden should be without a few clumps. The little pink *V. 'Coeur d'Alsace'* is also reliable and starts flowering as early as February.

The most floriferous of all the early violas to appear during mild winter spells is *V. florariensis*, which has flowers with intriguingly different expressions. Another enthusiastic self-seeder, it gives marvellous value, flowering from March to December or January. If you see it anywhere, grab it. Despite its fecundity, this fixed hybrid of the species *V. calcarata* is not often seen, though there is a mild resurgence of interest in violas and pansies which might see this and other old varieties available freely again.

Colonies of the native blue *Viola odorata* and the southern European *V. alba* can be established with garden violas at the foot of a hedge or around deciduous shrubs, where they will get all the winter light they need. Later on, when these kinds have stopped flowering, they will be shaded out by the advancing foliage of summer. A light sprinkling of flowers will appear sporadically from late autumn, followed by a great flush starting in February.

Pansies have coarser and larger flowers than violas but good strains of the winter pansies are nonetheless lovely, velvety things with honest, open faces that always meet your gaze with a smile. Like all the family, they require nothing more than good cultivation in rich, well-drained soil and a regular inspection for slugs, who are very partial to a bit of pansy. Greenfly and vine weevils are keen on them too, so be vigilant when choosing plants. If the plants are sticky, it's an aphid; if wilting, then it's either a lack of moisture or the dreaded vine weevil. By scratching away a good centimetre of the soil around the stem of a potted pansy, you should be able to see if there are any horrible off-white grubs, curled into a 'c' and feeding off its roots.

Pansies will grow in full sun or in shade and flower for months on end. Like their sisters the violas they're perennial but become leggy and unproductive after a season and are best replaced with fresh stock each year. The smaller-faced, wilder-looking violas, however, are even more tolerant and seed themselves about freely, even becoming naturalized in grass.

Pansies come in a huge range of colours, but pretty as they are individually, some of the random colour combinations they've been subjected to are terrifying. The important thing is to choose your colours carefully, either all tones of one colour or a carefully thought-out combination. Chinese yellow and red look well together, for example, and some of the bi-coloured pansies have their own in-built colour schemes, some of them beautiful. These are best grouped alone.

Tulips look beautiful when they soar and flower behind pansies in spring. Pansies spilling out of pots and containers near the house or in odd corners of the garden are a real joy in winter. If you want to have pots of pansies and nothing but pansies then the effect can be a bit flat. Try this simple, old-fashioned tiering trick to add a bit of height and shape. Take three sizes of complementary terracotta pots – one big, one medium and one smaller. Fill with heavy soil-based compost to act as ballast against the winds and plant generously around the edges of the biggest two. Jam the medium one into the centre of the first and then the baby one, fully planted up, into that, and you have a pyramid of pansies.

For the best visual impact, plant them in great masses of one colour, or tones of one colour, whether in tubs or running in streams through the open garden. Along with the smaller hardy geraniums, violas are perfect for edging and weaving roles. My mother-in-law is mad about violas and pansies of all kinds. She uses them massed at the feet of choice ivies trained up slender iron arches. She makes deep pools of different blues in places that catch the winter sun and threads fat ribbons of white, cream and pale yellows through dark, narrow borders planted with ferns and small bulbs.

Many years ago she gave me three varieties of the horned violet from the Pyrenees, *V. cornuta*: a pure white, an uncompromising bluey-mauve, and the old-fashioned hybrid 'Maggie Mott', which has silvery-mauve flowers with a cream centre. My clay back then was too heavy for poor old Maggie, who had been plucked in an untimely fashion from a free-draining loam, and she died quietly.

But the other two are still thriving, in much improved soil. I find

V. cornuta fantastically good for weaving itself up and through those roses with bare, ungainly legs. *V.* 'Jackanapes' is very cheerful, with three lower yellow petals and two chocolate brown above. Named after Gertrude Jekyll's pet monkey, it's a cheeky, bushy little plant, probably originating from a cross between a garden viola and the wild Heart's Ease pansy, *V. tricolor*, from which all garden varieties of pansy and viola originate. It is a martyr to slugs, and you could try giving it a collar of gravel to deter them. It flowers freely for months, from spring through summer, and reaches a height of nine inches.

Any ordinary, deeply dug and moderately rich loam, provided it is loose, gritty and moist, will suit the viola family. Heavy, unadulterated clay is not good for them, as the demise of 'Maggie Mott' demonstrated. A cool but not overly damp position in partial shade is best. They look wonderful with stone and often seed themselves in the edges of paving slabs.

Every two or three years they should be moved around or they could die out. I shake their seed capsules around the edges of beds and borders and find them quite obliging. If they are to stay in place for a third year, give them a liberal dressing of compost or rotted manure. If you look after them, they will reward you with much better flowers and stronger plants better able to withstand the depredations of slugs.

Violas can be propagated from seed, cuttings and root division. Cuttings can be taken from April to the end of October from short, stout vigorous growth, not wiry and hard runners which are useless. For early flowering, try propagating by division of roots in September. Seed sown in June should give flowers the following spring. All violas like to be deadheaded regularly, which prolongs flowering. A few favourite plants can be left to go to seed for collecting and resowing.

Hardy Geraniums

Once the intense freshness of spring has passed, and even the stately tulips are going over for another year, you may begin to notice emerging gaps in your planting scheme that you weren't anticipating. These can be filled with hardy annuals of varying heights this year, but for the future, you could consider the hardy geraniums, the cranesbills, for the job.

There are 140 species and 201 cultivars currently in existence, ranging in size from a few inches to four feet in height and spread. They are a generous and giving race of mainly herbaceous perennials with beautiful, understated flowers in shades of blue, white, pink, magenta and mauve from early summer to September, depending on type. By using different ones, their season can last at least ten if not twelve months, between their flowers and leaves, many of which are good in winter, whether it's the old foliage turning to reds or the new season's appearing. Most are good for ground cover and when their few needs are met they blend into the garden scene with a subtle grace and sympathy. Barring a really boggy situation, they will thrive in any reasonable soil, in sun, part shade or full shade. Some, like *G. phaeum* (the Mourning Widow), *G. nodosum* and *G. punctatum*, actually prefer full shade.

The Mourning Widow, so called because of its nodding, black-maroon flowers with reflexed petals, is a prolific self-seeder, especially in lawns and around the legs of other plants. Useful and rather mysterious under the shade of deciduous trees, it reaches a height of two feet and has an eighteen-inch spread. A good variation is the dark 'Lily Lovell'; *G.p. lividum* is a slate colour; and the white form, *G.p.* 'Album', is a real beauty.

There is still considerable confusion between the cranesbills (the flower stalks explain the common name) and the pelargoniums, a mainly tender relative of the *Geraniaceae* family, which also includes erodium, monsonia and sarcocaulon. A favourite cottage plant, geraniums were cultivated since the sixteenth century by noted botanists and herbalists, but many Victorians and Edwardians wouldn't give them garden room. Perhaps they were just too wild at heart for their bourgeois sensibilities.

While the good-natured geraniums were not at all showy enough for most Victorians, their only real fault is their lack of scent, always a bit of a disappointment in a flower. The exception is *G. macrorrhizum*, an utterly reliable, dense and weed-proof ground cover with clammy, aromatic leaves turning to give good autumn colour, despite being semi-evergreen. *G. macrorrhizum* is used in oil of geranium and cats don't like being near it. Of Mediterranean origin, it can cope with dry soil. Flowers in white, magenta ('Czakor' is good) and pale pink appear in early spring and carry on through to late summer.

For height and brilliance there's the somewhat raucous *G. psilostemon*, until lately called *G. armenium* (after its place of origin, Armenia). It reaches a height and spread of four feet and forms a great clump of well-cut, broad leaves which also take on a fine autumn colour. It is an arresting sight from June to September with dozens of intense, magenta-crimson flowers with striking black centres. It grows in sun or partial shade in any deep soil and usually needs some support, even if it's just a few obliging neighbours to lean on. Lovely in purple or grey groupings or with orange *Alstroemeria*, it also consorts well with blue campanulas and the later-flowering euphorbias.

G. wallichianum, a good front-of-border specimen, was brought back from the Himalayas in 1820. The oldest known garden form is 'Buxton's Variety', which likes moister soil and reaches one foot by three feet in sun or part shade. It produces a non-stop procession of Spode-blue flowers with large, white centres from the end of June.

Another one-footer with a slightly lesser spread is *G. himalayense* 'Grandiflorum'. Its violet-blue, veined flowers hover airily over daintily cut leaves which often assume brilliant autumn colouring. 'Irish Blue', with lighter blue flowers, is a form found at St Catherine's Park in Leixlip by Graham Stuart Thomas in the late 1940s. The same plantsman recommends using them in early summer, teamed with *Iris x flavescens* for a lovely effect.

The Bloody Cranesbill, *G. sanguinem*, is native from Donegal to the Caucasus and northern Turkey, with magenta to pink flowers for weeks in early summer, to a height of one foot. 'Album' is pure white and stretches to two feet. The low-growing *striatum* variety, usually pink, grows wild on the Burren in Co. Clare and has a very long flowering season. Though reputed to be rather tender, *G. maderense* (which does have a smell, and it's nasty) reaches an impressive one and a half metres and does well in our milder climate.

This is just a random selection; Johnson's Blue, *maculatum, pratense*, the native *sylvaticum*, *G. clarkei* and the sun-loving, nine-inch *G. riversleaianum* 'Russell Pritchard' haven't even been approached here. But along with old roses, their favoured companions, the hardy geraniums are enjoying a revival, with breeders working quietly in the background to provide as wide a choice of both as they can muster.

Pelargoniums

It's strange how things fall in and out of fashion and how slavishly a fashion victim will follow the dictates of a recognized guru. Gardening is no exception, except that instead of fashions changing for style reasons, as they do with hair and clothes, they seem to do so for purely snobbish reasons. As a result, good, reliable plants that have given years of loyal service are cast out into a kind of limbo for the horticulturally stained.

When a plant becomes 'common', that is, when the big, commercial nurseries propagate it and make it available to the masses, it immediately goes out of high fashion. Strange, really, as I said. Surely if something is good enough to want in the first place, it remains good forever, like houses, furniture and pictures. (People are a different matter.)

Limbo is where the pelargoniums, widely confused with geraniums, have been biding their time since they were cast out of the golden circle some time ago. Once the pride and joy of collectors, this native of South Africa has been rather messed about with by breeders, resulting in some pretty naff colours and combinations, which hasn't helped their reputation. But on the whole I rather like them, so I am pleased that at least the scented-leaved types are making a serious comeback.

If you want to be bang in the middle of high gardening fashion, get yourself some scented-leaved pelargoniums. There are lots to choose from, including, in alphabetical order, the following. *P. capitatum* is rose-scented and has rose and purple flowers. *P. citriodorum* has citron-scented leaves and white flowers. *P. crispum* smells of lemons and has rose flowers. The leaves of *P. fragrans* smell of nutmeg and its flowers are white and pink. *P. rachula* smells of balsam, reaches two to three feet and carries rose and purple flowers. All of the above grow to between two and three feet high.

Slightly taller, at three feet, is the peppermint-scented *P. tomento-sum*, with white flowers. Orange-scented are the leaves of *P.* 'Prince of Orange', while its flowers are pale mauve. Last and least, in that it only grows to a foot in height, is the fresh, apple-scented *P. odoratissimum*, with pure white flowers.

Pelargoniums are not reliably hardy, though I've seen them grown outside as hardy perennials in at least two places in Dublin. One is an enormous window-box on Fitzwilliam Square, where they have been putting on a fantastic display of scarlet for as long as I can remember. The other is climbing up the front of a red-brick house in Fairview, an area which has the benefit of mild sea air.

A perennial when grown in a cool greenhouse or conservatory, pelargoniums are happiest when in a soil consisting of loam, a little leaf mould and sand. Cuttings can be taken from July to September to flower the following year, readily rooting when temperatures reach 45 degrees Fahrenheit or more. To appreciate the fragrance, rub the leaves gently between your fingers, where it will linger on for some time.

Wallflowers & Camellias

Close your eyes and think of spring. After picturing the snowdrops, narcissi, scillas, tulips and other bulbs, what's missing? Ah, there it is, filling out the picture: old-fashioned, warm and comforting, it's the sweet daylight scent of wallflowers. Any time I've neglected to plant *Cheiranthus*, to give it the Latin moniker, I've bitterly regretted its absence in spring.

It is, as always, better to grow your own from seed, so you can choose your colours and are guaranteed clean stock. If you didn't, rush to a reputable retailer, where you may find some wallflowers in single colours instead of mixed. If mixed is all that's left, then try to find Persian Carpet, a mix of mainly pastels combined with lovely, dark velvety colours to create the effect suggested by its name. Pinch out the growing tips to encourage bushiness and don't buy them if they're weak and leggy. In garden-speak, to be 'leggy' is certainly not sexy.

Smaller varieties, less prone to legginess, are good in pots, and the Siberian wallflower, with its intensely sweet scent, makes a good low splash of clear orange and vivid gold. Wallflowers are not fussy as to soil, and, if given half a chance, are really perennials that will root in old walls, hence the name. As for the children's street song which begins 'Wallflowers, wallflowers growing up so high', the only really tall ones I've seen are in sheltered old gardens, where they flower year after year in the same place and are cared for in the same way as perennials.

Another perennial that is waiting to take its place in the limelight in my garden is the potted camellia. Mine is a *C. williamsii*, named after the Williams family of Caerhays Castle in Wales, and these have the advantage of casting off their own flowers when they've bloomed, which means you don't have the tedious task of dead-heading. If a camellia has been fed (it likes liquid tomato food) from spring to the end of July, and if it didn't suffer drought during the long summer, then by winter it should have swelling buds and shining green leaves. If it suffered, then the buds will be brown and dry and there'll be no flowers this time round. Don't despair. Nurse it and it may recover next year – I've seen miracles.

I've dragged mine out of a corner, given it plenty of rainwater from the bottom up, which it prefers, and, because camellias are root-tender, I've put down a layer of protective mulch. In this case the mulch is tea-leaves. The camellia is, in fact, a tea plant and loves nothing better than a strong pot of *cha*. It doesn't need any other food until spring, or it will make soft, sappy new growth vulnerable to frost. Morning sunshine on frosted camellias in winter can destroy them, so never place them facing east.

They don't mind shade at all, though in the coldest parts of the country it's wisest to have them facing south. The *C. reticulatas*, which are less reliably hardy than the *japonicas*, have the biggest, blowsiest flowers and are happy and safe by a north-facing wall. Another enemy of the potted camellia is the dreaded vine weevil, and a drench with a weak solution of Jeyes Fluid is recommended by fanciers. If looked after properly, there is no reason why a plant can't spend its entire life in a pot.

While debates rage as to the vulgarity of some of the more extravagant camellias – like Dumas's dying courtesan, *La Dame aux Camellias*, they are not always welcome in polite society – the actual pronunciation of the flower of Traviata is a contentious issue. Some say 'Cameelia'; I say 'Camellia', with a short 'e'. So which is correct? To illustrate why I use the short 'e', I'll tell you the origin of the name of this native of the Far East, and you can decide for yourself.

It was named in honour of a seventeenth-century Jesuit missionary who combined his religious work in the Philippines with his study of natural history. His name was Georg Joseph Kamel. That gives you a short 'e'. I rest my case.

Hellebores

What's in a name? Try asking the poor hellebore, which has suffered under its appellation for many years. 'Sounds hellish and boring,' is one worn joke, made by people who don't know its charms. As for *Helleborus foetidus*, the much-maligned Stinking Hellebore, which does wonderfully well in difficult places near deciduous trees and shrubs, it's a wonder it didn't just curl up and disappear long ago under such a cruel name. Add to that the same plant's dark, poisonous reputation and its association with depressing undergrowth where it never seemed to flower, and it's easy to see why they are not more widely grown.

The word hellebore, from the Greek, means something like 'to kill' (*hellin*) and 'food' (*borus*), which doesn't help its reputation particularly. But give the hellebores their common names of Christmas Rose and Lenten Rose and people react with oohs and aahs and are altogether more pleasant and positive about this good family, which offers sculpted flowers and classically poised, architectural foliage through the darkest days of winter and early spring.

Although hellebores have been in cultivation for hundreds of years, the true charms of this elevated member of the buttercup family (*Ranunculaceae*) have been a well-kept secret among the plant-collecting cognoscenti until fairly recently, when beautiful new hybrids of *H. orientalis* were produced by specialist breeders and began trickling through to mainstream garden centres.

Many people don't see the point of green flowers, and the perception that hellebores only come in green-on-green is still strong. In fact they come in a huge range of shadings, from pure white through pale yellow (rare) to pink, purple, slate, strange dark reds, almost black and a variety of mottled hues. When Vita Sackville-West wrote in praise of green flowers she singled out for special praise both *H.*

foetidus, with its perfect bells in bright, fresh apple-green, and *H. viridiflora*, a pure and rather brilliant green. With a few strokes of the pen, she started them back into fashion among her circle of acolytes, a fashion that has at last caught the fancy of the general public.

There are two types of hellebore: the truly herbaceous, which die back for a few months, and the evergreen, *H. corsicus, lividus, foetidus* and their numerous hybrid offspring, which produce a leafy stem one year and carry flowers at their apex the next. The flowers don't die as such but linger on and just seem to fade away slowly.

They are prone to a sort of blackspot disease of the leaves but are otherwise genetically sound. Just pick off the unsightly leaves and discard; besides preventing the spread of the blight, it will also give the flowers a better chance to show off their uncluttered beauty. No garden should be without a clump of hellebores in winter. If you go for different colours and types, they show up best if separated from each other a bit, rather than all bunched together.

Cultivation is not difficult. Most kinds will live in shade, or sun, planted in moist, leafy, retentive but reasonably drained soil that doesn't dry out during the summer. Their requirements are few – a good mulch of organic matter in autumn and again in February should do the trick, though they do benefit from an extra feed, particularly in liquid form, after flowering. I use diluted seaweed, for everything.

They say that the more you mollycoddle *H. niger*, the white Christmas Rose, the more elusive it becomes, rarely giving blooms early enough for the Christmas table. (Contrary to its Latin name, there is nothing black about it, except its roots.) All the hellebores like to be left alone once established. If you move or divide them, they could respond by going into a massive sulk for a couple of years. Many self-seed freely, and the seedlings, which can be moved away from the parent plant, could give you some interesting sports of your own.

It is probably better to buy them in flower so you can see exactly what you're getting. If you have something spectacular – like *H. niger* 'Potter's Wheel', with luminous white flowers up to five inches across, or 'St Brigid', a hybrid discovered in a castle in Co. Cork – it is better to propagate it by division. That way you're sure of getting an exact clone of the parent plant.

Seed can be bought, at a price, but fresh seed gathered at the optimum moment in May or June is generally more successful. The Corsican hellebore, also found in Sardinia and the Balearic Islands, is a handsome bushy cousin, with stout stems and beautiful tripartite greyish-green leaves like good leather, with prickly edges. Its pendent flowers of the palest green are produced in large clusters, up to about three feet in height and are lovely with early *Iris reticulata*. The Corsican group likes a sunny and well-drained spot.

Christmas Rose

The Lenten Rose belongs to the *H. orientalis* group, which has produced some stunning cultivars, now more widely available. While the Christmas Rose and the obliging *H. foetidus* are good for cutting, the Lenten Rose and some others are more temperamental. If you split their stems for a few inches on one side and plunge them into boiling water, they should last well. All hellebores dislike stuffy, over-warm rooms and should be taken out to an unheated place at night to cool down.

Independent, undemanding, handsome plants that between them flower from November to May, the hellebores are also valued for their longevity and capacity to smother weeds. See them early in the year, making an extraordinarily beautiful foil for snowdrops, aconites, crocuses, early irises and primroses, and you'll understand why they've taken the wider gardening world by storm.

Agapanthus

Elegant Edwardians loved agapanthus, the blue African lily, and grew them massed in pots for flowering outside in late July and August. A perennial, the South African lily takes its Latinized name from the Greek *agape*, meaning pure or unconditional love, and *anthos*, meaning flower. A member of the onion/lily family, the *Agapanthus* genus has at least ten species whose names still cause confusion among botanists.

Combining beauty with utility, agapanthus is manna in the late-summer garden. While its understated beauty alone earns it a place in the sun, its flowers (very lightly scented), in a palette of very good blues ranging to white and near-purple, are also adept at cooling down the strong upstart yellows which tend to dominate the garden in late summer. One of my best deep blues looks good growing near the bronzy-leaved, sulphurous yellow *Crocosmia*, 'Solfatare', which is a very well-behaved plant, unlike its cousin *Crocosmia crocosmiiflora* – the common Montbretia that is colourfully colonizing the country's hedgerows along with *Fuchsia magellicana*.

Agapanthus flower heads are borne in umbelliferous clusters on elegant stems. They are good for picking and last a long time in water. In the garden, the seed heads remain decorative for a long time after flowering. The tradition has been to drag them inside under cover for winter, but in fact most of them are pretty hardy. They come with both broad, evergreen strap leaves and narrower, grassier ones that are deciduous and die back in winter, leaving no trace above ground.

As a general rule, the wider the leaf the less reliably hardy the plant. When you consider that the broad-leaved, evergreen sorts grow in frost-free coastal regions and the deciduous types in moister, inland mountain areas, it's easier to understand their needs. If in doubt about the hardiness of any you have planted in the ground, protect them in winter with a thick mulch or covering of leaves, bracken or sacking.

A. africanus is not reliably hardy, though I have overwintered it outside in pots here in the city for the last few years. In the freezing weather at the beginning of 1996, its leaves did turn to mush, but it suffered no permanent damage and continues to be tucked away every winter in a corner of the yard where frost rarely reaches.

Coming from southern Africa, agapanthus are by nature sun lovers. In Ireland, you often see them flowering well enough but leaning right over as they strain towards our weaker sun. This is a pity, as it robs them of their noble stature and the chance to display themselves at their finest. Photographs of them growing *en masse* in the wild show them straight and tall, their heads in the sun. Most kinds lean, with the known exception of the *A. inapertus* clan, whose stems stay more or less erect. If you want them at their most thrilling, only a southern exposure is good enough for them. All the species appreciate fertile, moist but not soggy, waterlogged soil.

Slow enough to increase, they do eventually build up to vigorous clumps, ranging up to about four feet in height, depending on the species. There are two schools of thought on whether division is necessary to set them flowering freely. One says divide every few years, the other advocates leaving well alone. I haven't had mine long enough to decide, but I suspect it depends on the growing conditions and the surrounding competition. A couple of summers ago, I saw a shining example of the leave-well-alone school in a south-facing front garden on the Grand Canal in Dublin, which seemed to be filled entirely with blue agapanthus and nothing else – a fabulous sight set against the painted stucco of the Regency terraced house.

Either way, division is not an easy matter of teasing out the roots, as with many perennials. Even after a couple of years, they are hopelessly tough and entangled and need to be cut, a job best done with an old kitchen saw-knife, in spring. They can also be raised from seed. I tried, rather feebly, but had no success with the famous Headbourne Hybrids, introduced into general circulation in the '50s and '60s by Lewis Palmer when he distributed seed from his Winchester garden. But lots of other people have had great success with them over the years, giving rise to many named garden varieties from which to choose. Among those highly recommended are 'Lilliput', dark blue and not so tiny; 'Midnight Blue', raised at Slieve Donard and larger at two feet; 'Loch Hope', at four feet, a late-flowerer with large flower heads; 'Luly Palmer', a lovely light blue, at three feet; and 'Blue Giant'.

The white (*'Albus'*) which comes in for most praise among the hybrids is 'Alice Gloucester', an early flowerer with a large head, purplish in bud. 'Victoria', a creamy white, and 'Snowy Owl' are also highly rated. To start you off on your first engagement with the flowers of pure and unconditional love, try the species *A. campanulatus*.

Reliably hardy – though a mulch in winter in the coldest midland counties would be provident – this is a stalwart for the late summer garden. It flowers freely, albeit on rather flat rather than spherical heads, in lovely, soft shades of pale to deep blue. If planting *Agapanthus* in containers, use a good, free-draining loamy potting mix, such as a John Innes No. 1 formula. They thrive on benign neglect in winter and plenty of water plus a weekly liquid feed coming up to flowering time.

Clematis

Distinctive cousins of the yellow buttercup family (*Ranunculaceae*), and siblings to the Traveller's Joy or Old Man's Beard of the hedgerows, the genus *Clematis* comprises an enormous group of beautiful climbing shrubs and herbs, ranging from herbaceous plants little more than a foot high to woody climbers over fifty feet long.

Though fragrance cannot be taken for granted in a clematis, the evergreen *C. armandii* smells very good; *C. alpina* and its plumper cousin, *C. macropetala*, with nodding blue flowers, make up in grace what they lack in scent; and the unstoppable, almond-scented *C. montana* has flowers of pure white and shades of pink. In the warmest gardens there could even be a fifth for spring, the delectable, frost-shy *C. indivisa*, an evergreen with cupped blooms quite often cultivated in cool greenhouses. It needs an even warmer, cosier spot than the leathery-leaved *armandii*, because its buds appear so early in spring they're very vulnerable to frostbite.

There are clematis for all seasons and situations, with some of them, particularly the *orientalis* groups, making pretty silken seed heads which remain decorative long after flowering. Most of the climbing species support themselves by their leaf-stalks, which curl their way around anything slender within reach. The flower doesn't have true petals, but a coloured calyx made up of four to eight sepals.

All of them, including *montana* which will grow in the darkest, hardest places, like to have their feet shaded from the sun. This is easily achieved by placing flat stones or slates around the base or by planting something in front to shade them. They like a good, open, fairly rich loamy soil. Where lime or chalk is missing, it is wise to supply it or you could lose them. An annual mulch of well-rotted manure or garden compost, preferably in November, is beneficial, particularly on poor soils.

As for the vexed question of pruning, it depends on the type and when it flowers, which is why you should always keep the label. In fact, you should get yourself a special label box or drawer. It's fascinating to rummage through the old ones, rediscover the name of something you'd forgotten or wonder what happened to another plant long disappeared underground. The tangle an unpruned clematis gets itself into has been compared variously to a bird's nest, a dropsical mass and a disembowelled mattress. The trouble is, they can't all be pruned the same way, though some of the stronger types which have grown bare at base and tangled at the top can be safely cut hard back.

According to the expert clematis grower Christopher Lloyd, there are three basic pruning methods which the average gardener needs to know. (Remember, though, that flowering times can vary by a few weeks, depending on climate.) With the small-flowered species and their varieties which bloom in March, April and May (such as all of those mentioned in the second paragraph), cut out all shoots that have flowered immediately after flowering stops. All those large-flowered hybrids which start flowering before mid-June, e.g., 'Nelly Moser', 'Marie Boisselot', 'Ville de Lyon' and 'Lasurstern', should have their dead growth cut out completely in February or March; then separate and train the remaining shoots and shorten them back to the first pair of strong buds. Those that start flowering after mid-June, e.g., *C. tangutica*, *C. flammula*, 'Comtesse de Bouchard', *jackmanii* and 'Mme Edouard Andre', should have all shoots cut back hard in February or very early March, to a strong pair of buds no more than three feet above ground.

If you want those clematis in the first group to cover a large area, there's no need to prune them annually, just very hard, once every four or five years. Their vigour is such that to keep them within bounds in a small space an annual haircut is needed. Because these flower on shoots made the previous year, cutting them in early May gives them enough summer time to grow lots of new shoots for flowering next year. If you leave pruning until winter, then every shoot you cut loses you literally dozens of spring blossoms.

When planting a clematis – and they are widely available now as pot-grown specimens – it's wise to take into account the trojan work it is expected to do, covering walls and arches, clambering up and through trees and climbing roses or scrambling over large shrubs, year after year. Once it is planted, it's not even safe to fork around its roots; all you can do to help it on is give it nourishing top-dressings.

So prepare your ground well. Dig a hole eighteen to twenty-four inches square and the same deep. Lay the good topsoil to one side, removing any useless, impermeable subsoil and laying a layer of grit or shingle at the bottom, on top of sloping tiles if drainage is a real problem. Fill the hole with a can full of water to see how fast it drains. Start filling in the hole, using really generous amounts of rotted manure or garden compost at the bottom. Then add the topsoil mixed with plenty of peat or used potting compost for aeration, and a couple of handfuls of a slow-acting fertilizer like the dreaded bone-meal, and pack it down firmly with your heel as you fill.

Plant before the hole is completely filled, about an inch or so deeper than the clematis is growing in its pot. This helps guard against wilt, which can strike the healthiest of plants completely out of the blue. Firm in really well, using your fists with all your body weight behind them and water really well. Top dress with more stuff and away she goes, the well-named Queen of the Climbers.

Borage

It's a marvellous thing to discover something for yourself, even if you subsequently learn that others have got there first. This happened to me with borage (*Borago officinalis*), the hairy-leaved annual herb with flowers of the purest blue which you sometimes see floating prettily on the surface of summer cocktails and claret cups at smart parties, or decorating salads in equally smart restaurants.

One fine morning some years ago, after a surfeit of the said summer cocktails the evening before, I was walking in the garden to restore myself and wishing my puritan streak would allow me resort to a hair of the dog that bit me so I could get on with life. But the problem with cocktails is that there are various dogs involved, and besides, most people won't tell you the truth about the breeds used in making their mongrel mixes, so a specific cure is out of the question, even for the libertarian.

The only ingredient I had recognized the night before was the borage flowers so, since the garden was awash with their blue stars at the time, I started eating my way through them. They were juicy, and invigorating, and the result was amazing: within an hour or so a cure was effected. Since then I have learned a lot about borage, not least that it is the main ingredient in starflower oil, the expensive oil that my neuroscientist friend says is a must for keeping the brain primed, and is a great healer if taken regularly after a bang on the head.

That's modern scientific research, but it ties in neatly to some of what the ancient herbalists said all along, that borage is good for the mind. They also claimed that it brings courage to the nervous heart, dispels melancholy and induces euphoria, which could explain why it's such a good hangover cure. Borage was rumoured to be the nepenthes of Homer, who drank it steeped in wine 'to bring about absolute forgetfulness', though probably the wine had something to do with that.

I could go on and on about the medicinal properties claimed for borage, both its flowers and leaves: diuretic; anti-inflammatory; good for bronchitis, catarrh, congested membranes, pleurisy, rheumatism, the frantic and the lunatic.

The borage (*Boraginaceae*) family is a large one, to which forget-me-nots (or 'Le ne m'oubliez pas ou Vergisseinnicht'), comfrey, viper's bugloss, the hilariously large and leaning *Echium pininana*, lungwort (*Pulmonaria*), hound's tongue (*Cynoglossum*), oysterplant (*Mertensia*) and the lesser honeywort – there is a beautiful and much sought-after purpureum type – all claim kinship.

Once you've sown borage you've got it for life. It seeds itself around, sometimes in the perfect place, other times not, but you can just yank it out and eat the young leaves in salad, or transplant it anywhere except in deep shade. Strong, clear blues among flowers are quite rare, so borage's pendent clusters of cobalt stars and soft, grey-green leaves add up to a highly decorative plant that's always welcome.

Unless you can find the miniature version – which I have – it is not a good idea to use it for edging paths if you like things very tidy. Borage grows to three feet high. Upright and stout at first, it flops and sprawls about when in full flower. You can cut it back when necessary, however, without harming the plant. In fact borage is so hardy that, though it is an annual, it can come through the winter unscathed. Even now as I write, during a mild spell in the latter half of January, there are a few flowers threatening to open. In the interests of research, I picked and chewed a few young leaves and found them creamy and slightly stimulating on the palate. Full of minerals, they'll make a good addition to winter salads.

Borage will grow in moist soils, but it prefers a loose, stony soil with some sand in it. Because of its drooping habit, it is good planted on banks or in hollow walls where its lovely flowers can be seen at eye level. It can be effective too around the edges of pots or under roses and fruit trees. Both its flowers and leaves contrast well with copper or purple-leaved shrubs, and bees love it for honey.

Borage is thought to be native to North Africa, central Europe, the Mediterranean and the Middle East, but is now naturalized in North America and on these islands. Sow the seeds outdoors in spring where they are to flower, or in drills for transplanting like any other salad crop. Drop two or three seeds to each quite shallow hole, preferably in well-drained, ordinary garden soil. For a succession the first year, you can make another sowing in midsummer. Occasionally pinching off the ends of branches will encourage bushiness.

A white-flowered variety, which I don't recall ever seeing in the flesh, is also available, and could have its uses as a gap-filler in a restrained planting scheme, such as a cool white, silver and grey border. Borage blooms fully from June to September and sporadically at other times. Its name is thought to be derived from the Latin *corago*, which means 'I bring courage to the heart'.

Culinary Herbs

The good news is that growers have cottoned on and provided Irish cooks with an unprecedented range of fresh herbs, never available before in our shops. The bad news is that they cost so much for so little. A few sprigs of this and that, including mint for heaven's sake, retail at somewhere around £1. After you unwrap the tacky clingfilm and examine the booty in its flat little plastic tray, it's almost always a disappointing amount and never enough if you're cooking for a crowd.

Anyone who eats at home and doesn't grow a few culinary herbs is either very rich or only uses parsley and thyme from Moore Street, Dublin, where the dealers still throw in huge bunches with the vegetables, mostly for free. But what about the sage for stuffings, the rosemary for lamb, the prodigious amount of dill needed for making gravadlax during the salmon season, the huge handfuls of fresh coriander needed for salads, soups and Eastern cooking?

Even if you are very rich, you are deprived if your world doesn't include the benediction bestowed by the merest brush with a lavender bush, lemon balm or pot of basil. Not all herbs are culinary, however, and some, though medicinal, are poisonous if used indiscriminately. Some are merely decorative, like *Nepeta* (catmint), which is beautiful as well as addictive for cats.

There are cats who come from all over the city and queue up in a friend's front garden to take their turn at lying and rolling in the catmint, chewing and eating it until it is all used up. Once they discovered it in the front, they were unstoppable and have now destroyed the catmint in the back garden as well. You could say 'not in my back yard', but it's a marvellous perennial, making great swathes of downy, soft grey foliage topped by blue flowers in summer – and a later flush if you cut it back.

There's a lot of sweet talk about the properties of herbs, but some of them are thugs, like the mighty colonizers the mints, the towering inferno that is lovage in its prime, and the promiscuous seeders, borage and salad burnet. You can grow herbs in formal beds or patterns with strong edges, which contain the sprawlers and spreaders and leave a good outline in winter, or plant them in any suitable site among flowers, shrubs and vegetables. One thing that most people agree on is that they should be planted near the kitchen door, for handy picking in foul weather.

EIGHT EASY HERBS

PARSLEY (*Petroselinum crispum*): Indispensable and full of iron. Does in sun or semi-shade and lasts for up to eighteen months, after which the roots can be added to soups and stocks. The curly moss type makes an excellent soft edging. Loose-leaf Continental parsley is just as easy to grow and many think its flavour superior. Parsley is said to deter greenfly if planted under roses.

Good Friday is a traditional day for the first sowing; a kettle of boiling water poured along the drill is supposed to speed germination, which is notoriously slow, sometimes taking six to eight weeks. Sow fast-growing radish mixed with it for almost instant gratification. A second sowing in July or August will give good winter picking. Parsley, chewed raw after eating garlic, helps dispel its strong odour.

SAGE (*Salvia*): The common grey, narrow-leaved sage, which looks good all year, has pretty flowers and extraordinary flavour. Singers use an infusion as a throat gargle for its antiseptic qualities. Purple sage is very decorative, but some types never flower and the flavour is inferior. Both are hardy perennials which can be pruned to shape. Clary (known in some circles as 'housemaid's armpits') and Painted Sage are biennials with good, bicoloured flowers.

Clary likes sweet, stony soil in full sun. Perennial salvias are easily grown from cuttings or by pegging down a branch, making a slit underneath and securing it to the ground with a piece of wire and heaping a bit of soil over it. Sage can usually be picked all year round.

ROSEMARY (*Rosmarinus*): If this grows well in your garden, the saying goes that there's a strong woman in the house (ditto parsley). One favourite is the fine architectural form of Miss Jessop's Upright, which makes an elegant small feature or medium-sized hedge and is very hardy. Give it a mild spot out of buffeting winds with some sun, preferably lots. Horizontal, sprawling rosemary looks good making its way down the walls of a raised bed. 'Sissinghurst' and 'Fota' have good blue flowers. Rosemary is said to strengthen the brain and memory and an infusion used as a rinse on dark hair is an effective conditioner.

THYME (*Thymus*): Indispensable in cooking with many medicinal uses, including the use of wild thyme essence as an antibiotic, for chest ailments in particular. Loves to be baked in the same sweet, arid soil as all herbs of Mediterranean character. Creeping thymes are used to make aromatic lawns and garden seats. Blooms from May to September and is easily grown from cuttings and seed. Gets leggy and should be replaced after a few years.

CORIANDER: Indian, Thai, Vietnamese, Chinese, Greek, you name it, many of the world's great cuisines call for pungent *Coriandrum sativum* by the handful, though those countries tend to have it growing as a virtual weed. The seeds, harvested in the autumn, are an aromatic digestive stimulant and an excellent kitchen spice. The problem is growing this erect annual well, so that it makes lots of leaf. Sow in May in good soil in sun and keep well watered to encourage a leafy base.

BASIL: A sun worshipper to its scented soul, sweet basil curls up its toes outdoors in most Irish summers, but it's always worth a try. A little edging row of *Ocimum basilicum*, making a ribbon along a bit of sunny, well-drained border, will supply you until autumn. Keep a few in pots for winter and to give away. I find bush basil the hardiest and as tasty as the larger-leaved varieties, though not so good for making pesto. Basil can be frozen in ice cubes.

MINT: People are always going on about the perils of giving mint its head in the open ground. 'It takes over,' they warn. 'Put it in a bucket with a hole in the bottom and it can't escape,' they advise like security consultants. Poor *Mentha*, of which the most useful to me are Peppermint (*Mentha x piperita*), for stomach-calming tea and ice-cream, and Apple Mint (*Mentha rotundifolia*), for mint and yoghurt sauces.

If you plant mint in a bucket the poor thing is often forgotten, never watered in a drought and vulnerable to attack from pests. Give mint its head to a certain extent, keeping it within bounds in the open garden with broken slates pushed well down around it. If it gets too invasive just yank it out until you're satisfied it's not going to go where it has no business. Pineapple Mint is so decorative it's grown as a front-of-border plant. Mints are perennial and most of them die back completely in winter.

LOVAGE: Another perennial herb with a reputation as a romper. Likes a moist spot and will tolerate some shade. An herbaceous plant with a cylindrical, hollow stem up to forty inches, its large, dark-green divided leaves have an aromatic, yeasty odour which livens up summer salads. Clusters of small, yellow flowers in June and July are followed by small, aromatic seeds. It has both culinary and medicinal uses and is ornamental in a coarse sort of way. Propagation is by seed when it's fresh in late summer or by root division in early spring.

Exotics

A growing number of people are rallying to the fashionable green call to go native by planting indigenous Irish species. Fortunately, the idea hasn't caused us to lose our sense of proportion. Of course it's important to plant native flora and encourage native wildlife, but with our welcoming climate it would be madness to deprive ourselves of the company of exotic strangers.

These beauties have been welcome guests on the Irish garden scene for centuries, and, in some famous cases, have interbred with the native flora to produce spectacular offspring. Our undying interest in growing foreign plants was illustrated recently by the record numbers who flocked to Wexford from every corner of Ireland to hear a lecture entitled 'The World in My Garden', given by the eminent collector, author, broadcaster and plantsman Roy Lancaster.

Organized by the Wexford Garden & Flower Club (which has over 260 members, many of them formidable gardeners), the mid-week, mid-afternoon lecture, at £10 a throw in aid of charity, completely packed out the conference room at the Ferrycarrig Hotel, which is about the size of a large ballroom. There must have been about 500 people, men and women of all ages, some of them with famous gardens of their own but all listening attentively for hours on end.

Geography, said Roy Lancaster, was never his strong subject until he became interested in plants, where they come from and what growing conditions suited them. Geography came alive for him as he began to hunt them down in their native habitats and collected their seed to grow on in various botanical institutes and in his own quite small garden in Hampshire, where he grows a truly catholic collection on acid Bagshot sand interspersed with pockets of clay.

At least five countries should be represented in even the humblest garden, he said, while a larger garden should have upwards of fifteen (or was that fifty?) countries on its books. On looking around my own small garden the next day, it was a relief to find myself still counting after ten. The countries of Africa north and south, New Zealand, Australia, China, India, Japan, Chile, Brazil, Mexico, Spain, Madeira, the Canary Islands, North America, New Guinea, Russia – all these and more were present and correct.

Maybe Roy Lancaster said fifteen in small gardens and fifty in large? Because now that I've been inspired to count them, I'd say that five is a very modest number to aspire to, even for the newest gardener or those cultivating a tiny space. More of a challenge would be to have five different nationalities all performing at the same season. For example, many of the familiar autumn stalwarts, things we take for granted as belonging to the Irish garden at this time of year, are not remotely native. Five good plants still going strong in my autumn garden are asters (eastern U.S., except for the shrubby kinds which hail mainly from southern Africa); Dahlias (Mexico and Central America), correctly pronounced 'Daahlia' after a M. Dahl, even if it does sound a bit affected; kaffir lilies and *Schizostylis* (southern Africa); and the utterly familiar chrysanthemums (from the Arctic, Russia, China, Japan).

There are more: fuchsias from Central and South America and New Zealand; salvias, which are widely distributed around temperate and tropical regions, though not in very hot and humid areas; nerines (southern Africa); abutilons; certain varieties of sorbus or mountain ash; hebes (New Zealand, Australia, New Guinea); and potato vines, one of which, *Solanum jasminoides 'Alba'* (Brazil), is flowering beautifully this season. So you see my point: it's easy to have the world in your garden at any time of the year.

Not quite so easy is relying on the Irish natives to give a good year-round show, unless you decide to go for massed planting in the wild style or collecting alpines, of which we have many good ones. Beeches love Ireland and we love beeches, being particularly fond of using them for hedging. But though so familiar, even they are not at all native. Their seed capsules floated up the Wash and Humber in south-east England about 10,000 years ago, during a melt in the last

Ice Age. Alas, they fell at the first hurdle and never made it across the channel. It was only in the eighteenth century that beech, *Fagus sylvatica*, was introduced to Ireland, where it liked the climate and soon spread itself around.

In search of five Irish species I took another walk around my garden. Not so easy. Number one would have been the beautiful old blackthorn that used to hang over from a neighbour's garden and give us sloes in winter, but it has been cut down. (Blackthorn wood is used for making the shillelagh, which an American professor of pharmacology once described as 'an ancient Hibernian tranquilizer'.)

The evergreen Killarney strawberry tree, *Arbutus unedo*, a true Hibernian with red bark, flowers and strawberry-shaped fruits, can be number one instead. Blue-eyed grass, *Sisyrinchium angustifolium*, makes two.

I don't even have an Irish spurge, *Euphorbia hyberna*, though I do have a few native ferns, and a very pretty multicoloured wild pea grown from seed collected in Donegal. There are Irish wood anemones under the bay tree in spring, pale mountain avens (*Dryas octopetala*), spring gentian (*Gentiana verna*), ivy-leaved toadflax and valerian. Next year there may be some self-seeded shamrock, *Trifolium dubium*, recognized as the badge of Irish nationality since the late seventeenth century but suffering indignities at the hands of the state in these changing times. That's five and more (whew!), but it's a poor show for Ireland on my sixteen perches if you discount the weeds.

Alpines

Writing in 1908, Reginald Farrer, father of the twentieth-century rock garden, warned that one must go very cautiously when dealing with alpine plants, calling them 'the perverse little people of the hills'. Perverse because they don't follow the normal rules and are often difficult to please. Little because dwarfed by the harsh climatic conditions of their natural habitats.

Such a description does not, of course, extend to the alpine specialists themselves, though this dedicated group of growers, daunting like all experts, does have a formidable reputation in gardening circles, being commonly perceived as finicky, difficult, demanding and sometimes as easily miffed as their chosen subjects. When you consider the lengths to which alpine enthusiasts will go to titivate a truly minuscule specimen to show standards, the hours and days spent fiddling about with tweezers and nail scissors, the little glass umbrellas on sticks they construct to keep the rain off their most prized specimens and the sheer depth of their specialist knowledge, it is understandable that the outsider should be somewhat in awe of them.

This reputation rather amuses the members of the Alpine Garden Society (AGS), who number about 150 in Ireland. During my two brief encounters with some of them, they proved an exceptionally friendly and normal bunch of enthusiasts, with a keen interest in the broader horticultural canvas. Though rivalry, jealousy and showing off are endemic in gardening circles, the alpinists are helpful and generous with their trade secrets, and particularly keen to spread the word among newcomers and novices.

This struck me last year when I went to their annual plant sale and show, and again when chatting after a recent, very entertaining lecture on the flora of Narnaqual and South Africa. Some of the showpieces, from mountains and meadows around the world, were truly spectacular. Though some alpines are a perfectly reasonable size, 'little treasures' are in the majority, with some of them so tiny that the thought of being responsible for them is terrifying. Putting any of them down to take their chances in the wilds of the average garden is unthinkable. They would, of course, be swallowed up straight away.

The word alpine can be widely interpreted to include all plants, including hardy perennials and bulbs, that grow naturally on high land. They fringe the fields of snow and ice of the mountains and often barely have time to flower before they are again buried deep in snow. No taller plants can survive in those conditions so the alpines flourish without competition. Luckily for us in this cool, northern climate, these conditions are not always essential for their growth and many plants growing in the Alps and other high mountain places are found on much lower ground here, for example on the limestone of the Burren in Co. Clare, where an extraordinary range, normally found in diverse regions, all flourish together.

While some rare and more difficult alpines need their own alpine houses to survive – simulating snow-melt at the roots and a sun-scorched and wind-raked atmosphere above ground – many of these exquisite plants are suitable for growing in rock beds in the garden, their chief demand being for sharp drainage.

Alpines possess the charm of endless variety and include such diverse things as tiny orchids, moss, ferns, lilies, bluebells, saxifrages, evergreen shrubs perfect in shape, leaf and fruit but so small that a glass thimble would house them, delicate little gentians and primulas and big toughies like arabis and aubrietia.

A rock garden, or even a small rock bed, simulates a mountain scree and most definitely has nothing in common with the average 'rockery' seen in front gardens, scathingly described by Reginald Farrer thus: 'In some old corner you rigged up a dump of broken cement blocks, and added bits of stone and fragments of statuary. You called this "The Rockery" and proudly led your friends to see it, and planted it all over with Periwinkle to hide the hollows in which your Alpines had promptly died.'

House-plants

Indoor plants make good companions, especially in winter when frosts have reduced most of the garden to mush. New gardens without a mature framework can look particularly bare and depressing. Unless you have planned for winter surprises, there will be nothing much to admire outside until the first stirrings of spring bring a rush of ecstasy coursing through the veins.

I'm ashamed to say it, but in the fine weather house-plants and their needs make me slightly impatient. Even the most gorgeous of them become a bit of a nuisance when there is so much excitement beckoning outdoors. Somehow they seem superfluous then, and feeding, tweaking and watering them is a chore performed grudgingly and erratically. Any that will tolerate it just get bunged outside for the six best months to take their chances. Cacti and succulents have responded to this harsh treatment by flowering profusely and repeatedly, but I nearly killed a lovely young plumbago (Cape Leadwort) one cold summer, which was a humbling experience. Neglect is so rampant around here that it's amazing they don't all just die in despair at their harsh, loveless life. In fact, such is the good and tolerant nature of most house-plants that they survive the most appalling and unnatural conditions. Even if they never get the opportunity to grow to their full potential they continue on with their job of making houses and offices safer, cleaner and happier places to be. If they do have a good life, then their beauty is a bonus. Large, lush specimens with good architectural foliage create a dappled, jungly shade and can make a hall or room restful, soothing and slightly mysterious.

Modern offices and some homes, where opening windows is considered an alien, anti-social concept, are heavily polluted with poisonous gases, such as formaldehyde, benzene and trichloroethylene. These gases come from things like polythenes, plastics, foam insula-

tion, glues, varnishes, inks, oils, detergents and even synthetic car-
pets.

Dry, stale air, little natural daylight, computers – all of which
could well apply to a child's room – lead to headaches, rashes, dry
skin, irritated eyes, blocked sinuses and a persistent feeling of not
being quite well. Many easy indoor plants have the ability to change
all that by gobbling up unwanted toxins, filtering them and convert-
ing the carbon dioxide we exhale back into oxygen. So talking to
plants is good good not only for them, but for us too.

Scientists have proven that Sick Building Syndrome (SBS), the
modern disease spread by bad architecture, can be cured with just one
suitable plant for every hundred square feet of space. That would be
a bit mean to a plant, to put it all on its own in such a big room:
plants like the company of others and usually look better in groups.

In the vanguard of the pollution-fighters are some of the most
common and easily cultivated of house-plants. The ubiquitous but
obliging spider plant (*Chlorophytum comosum*) and Mother-in-Law's
Tongue (*Sanseviervia trifasciata*), which has a sharp quality that
would not look out of place in the most modern room, are two of the
formaldehyde addicts that will do well in warm, dried-out spaces.

Tropical plants with lush foliage need humidity and low natural
light to thrive as they do in their jungle homes. Most new centrally-
heated offices are indeed low on natural light but also have stick-dry
air. The plants will sort this out and save everybody the misery and
expense of being sick. Stand the plants in trays of damp pebbles and
they will grow well, if not quite so enormous as they would in their
natural setting.

It's been a well-kept secret for years, but the common outdoor ivy
in all its forms is a benzene binger. So too is the unreal-looking Peace
Lily (*Spathiphyllum*), which looks like an Arum and has a flat, oval
spathe that comes in white, red and pink. These two sniff out their
sources of benzene like bloodhounds, though their supply has dwin-
dled in recent years since cigarette smoke, a reliable source, has been
banned in most public buildings.

Boston fern, the dwarf date palm (*Phoenix roebelenii*) and

chrysanthemums are other good fellas for gobbling up noxious, invisible gases. For the lavatory, try the lady palms and yuccas, which can absorb ammonia and its odours. House-plants reduce fungi, dust and other airborne bacteria. They also cut down noise levels and lend a peaceful hush to a place.

By the time house plants reach the supermarkets and garden centres they could already be dying, having been through a series of sudden, stressful shocks. Grown and cossetted in greenhouses and polytunnels under controlled conditions, their first knock is from the cold when they are shifted out for transportation. If a tropical plant is on display outside in the freezing wind, don't buy it: chances are it's not long for this world.

Pot chrysanthemums are the best survivors among the seasonal flowering plants. In spring they can be planted out, where they will outgrow the dwarfing hormones they've been treated with and grow on for years at their true, taller height. Buy solid-looking ones with no sign of wilt and with their buds just beginning to show colour. Keep in cool temperatures and keep the compost moist but not wet.

Azaleas are rhododendrons by another name and are happiest in cool woodland. Life in a pot takes some adjusting to, so it's best to buy a big, established one, with most of the buds closed and juicy leaves that show no sign of dropping. Keep it cool, humid, semi-shaded and moist, maybe in the hall, and it will flower for months. Never give it tap water but do add some tea and the odd bit of tomato feed to its favourite tipple, rainwater.

I'm constantly barraged with questions about ailing house-plants, mostly yuccas, and resort to my only reference book on the subject, by Dr D.G. Hessayon, a bestseller from a man who has produced a whole stable of bestselling 'Expert' books. While it has its uses, and refers to a huge range of plants, I have never liked it. It reads as if written by an automaton. Plants are treated as problems. Its tone put me off house-plants for years after I first consulted it.

So it was with great interest that I listened to a botanist called Paul Simons talking passionately on the radio last week about how to make house-plants feel at home. What he was saying, about understanding how house-plants live in their wild habitats, was so sensible – and downright moving – that I rushed into town to buy his and co-author John Ruthven's book, *Potted Histories*. While not nearly so comprehensive in its plant list as Dr Hessayon's bestseller, dealing as it does with only 108 of the commoner species, *Potted Histories* takes you much further into the heartland of plant life, and brings out the carer in you, determined to make life glorious for the straggly specimens orphaned in your house.

'Did you know', Simons and Ruthven ask, 'that your kitchen can be like a tropical rainforest, the hallway like the dark undergrowth on a spartan mountainside, and that a south-facing window compares to an Arizona desert?' They deal with the myths and legends, e.g., feeding plants cigarette ash (phosphates good, tobacco poison), beers and other alcohol (plants get hangover, not so good); talking to them (good, they need the gas, or carbon dioxide, for photosynthesis); playing music (good, if male voice choir or female solo) and stroking them (good, Japanese farmers stroke their sugar beet seedlings, and aphids don't like it).

A Fool for Raspberries

There's a late Italian Renaissance painting showing women talking, reading and sewing in an achingly fresh, perfectly square room full of dappled light and shade. Their bower, about twelve feet by twelve, is open to the sky and the walls are made entirely of raspberry canes in full leaf, growing twelve feet high. In reality, raspberries reach to about eight feet, but these were planted in a hollow, dry-stone wall, giving them a head start of four feet. They were trained vertically – as is proper – and laced through a wooden lattice affair, which could be bamboo. Gardens were taken very seriously in Renaissance Italy, and no doubt the walls were perfectly gauged to give shelter from the wind at sitting height.

Ever a fool for raspberries, this is an idea I'm determined to copy somewhere, some time, when the opportunity arises. One can quickly become accustomed to a way of life that includes feasting for weeks on freshly picked organic raspberries, with or without sugar and cream; or always having the best of raspberry jam for toasted bread and muffins, or for scone and sponge-cake fillings – enough raspberry jam to hold out until the marmalade oranges sail in from Seville in January. In our climate a raspberry bower is not at all unrealistic. The raspberry is a cool-climate plant and does very well in gardens as far north as Scotland and even Shetland, where I've seen it thrive in sheltered hollows. A sunny or lightly shaded position in rich, moist, free-draining soil dug with plenty of organic matter, suits it well.

Planted three inches deep and fifteen inches apart in neat rows and trained on wires stretched taut between two stout wooden posts, raspberries make good, clear divisions within the garden and become elegant screens when in leaf. They can be used to make tall, slender hedges beside paths or tied to groups of canes arranged in different shapes. Their shallow roots are easily damaged, but herbs, mint, strawberries and small annuals and perennials flourish at their feet.

Most canes have a horizontal, L-shaped root which should be planted facing along the row. If the ground is heavy, break it up well, and ensure good drainage with plenty of grit. If your soil is light, bulk it up with lashings of organic matter. Remove perennial weeds before you plant. Trying to remove deep-rooted dandelions and bindweed when the raspberries are established is nearly impossible without damaging their shallow roots.

A thick annual mulch of rotted manure, straw, compost or even grass mowings will give them the strength to concentrate on producing fruit. I only water mine in terribly dry weather when the berries are ripening, and a couple of times a year I give them some fresh potash, taken straight from the fireplace in the sitting-room where we keep a wood fire burning most evenings.

Summer-fruiting raspberries start cropping in late June or early July, but you can prolong the ecstasy until the first frosts by having a few canes of the autumn-fruiting variety. Expect between eight and twelve ounces of fruit from each plant. Not all varieties of raspberries taste wonderful. Some are watery and rather sour. Look out for Glen Moy (early), Malling Jewel (mid-season), Malling Promise (very early) and Heritage (autumn), which are among the best. Golden and black varieties exist and are reputed to have a distinctive flavour, but I've never tasted them.

Fig Trees

Since ancient times figs have caused controversy. The Zen masters of macrobiotics warn that a man with a fig tree in his garden will be morally and physically weakened by eating the fruits, which are so excessively yin that no amount of yang food will balance them. The classical Greeks, on the other hand, were great fans of *Ficus carica*. Pliny the Elder wrote: 'Figs increase the strength of young people and preserve the elderly in better health and make them look younger, with fewer wrinkles.'

The other thing about figs is that people either love them or just couldn't give a (ahem) fig about them. We're talking here about fresh figs, picked and eaten straight from the tree when they are just bursting with ripeness. The sensation bears no resemblance to eating the dried fruit. I once sat under a couple of wall-trained trees in a relative's garden in Andalucia and gorged myself, eating every fig that ripened there throughout August.

They had no ill effects, laxative or otherwise, so I'm running with Pliny the Elder and planting a fig this year, now that I've acquired a suitably large and sunny wall to train it against, courtesy of the neighbour's new studio. This is the best way to grow them in Ireland, with the reflected heat of the wall giving them an extra chance to ripen in August and September. Grown as free-standing trees, their exotic foliage creates a lush Mediterranean ambience, but the yield is unreliable, often negligible.

Grown in pots, they can be trained as fans or standards and moved indoors in winter, where, with heat, they'll give three crops a year, as opposed to one outdoors. But potted figs, while pretty, are a lot of trouble, needing constant tweaking, pruning and watering. Grown against a sunny west- or south-facing wall, however, they thrive on neglect and a harsh, stony diet, including limey builder's rubble, though good drainage is essential.

All figs resent the knife and untrained trees can be allowed their head. Wall-trained specimens look wonderful when allowed to grow huge and handsome, but some judicious pruning and tying-in will be necessary. Feeding is out after planting, unless the tree is absolutely failing to regenerate itself at the base. It's a perfect plant for sheltered urban gardens, being tough enough to withstand the onslaught of children and dogs.

They used to say you should restrict the fig's roots by planting it in an old leather doctor's bag. Most people don't have one handy and settle for a paved yard, or put a solid layer of stones or a slab of concrete at the bottom of the planting hole. Rich living and an unrestricted root run encourages lush foliage at the expense of fruit. When pruning, cut from the bottom up. The sap released, probably in revenge, seems harmless until it dries on the skin, where it can cause itching and burning.

Good outdoor varieties include the hardy and reliable 'Brown Turkey', which gives an early, heavy crop of moderate size. The fruit is sweet and rich, with red flesh and purple-brown skin. In a good year the slightly more tender 'Brunswick', known as the 'Madonna' until it was renamed for George I of England, bears the biggest and most luscious fruit. Its deeply indented leaves are larger, too, and it has no objection to covering a very large wall, if that's what you want it to do.

Self-fertile, the fig needs no companion and suffers little from pests and diseases, but it does need constant watering in dry weather. Try to keep the soil evenly moist as a sudden soak in drought conditions can cause the fruit to split. A non-nutritious mulch at the beginning of summer helps. Watch every day as the fruit ripens and then, just after it hangs its head on the stalk, when the skin is striped with juicy slits and the flesh inside is eager for release, you reach up and, with a gentle twist of the wrist, pick it and eat it on the spot.

The Pleasures of a Lemon Tree

The first time I saw a lemon tree in all its glory was in the garden of a house in the Alpes Maritime above Nice. The woman of the house was so taken with my youthful delight in its charms that she presented me with a basket of its ripe fruits, nestling among glossy, aromatic citrus leaves, to take home to Ireland. The taste of them, the smell of them, gave me intense pleasure for months afterwards. Smitten, I resolved that when I grew up I would have my own lemon tree, and live happily ever after.

Now, after all these years, I have just bought one and my enthusiasm knows no bounds, even though I will have to share the cool but sunny end of my kitchen with it until the last frosts have gone next year. Only nine months old and called a Meyer's Lemon, it is sitting small and pretty in its pot, with two perfect fruits hanging gracefully from its dark boughs.

The fruits on a Meyer's are thin-skinned, juicy, and sweeter than most. During its twelve-month cycle it produces hundreds of fragrant white flowers about one inch in size, and you will often see both fruit and blossom at the same time. About 60 per cent of the male flowers fall off but all the females produce, so they have to be culled when the fruits are small, leaving only a few to a cluster. You either cut with a sharp knife or secateurs, or gently twist off the fruits.

If you treat it really well, each little tree will give you fifteen to twenty big, juicy, organic lemons three times a year. If you don't pick them but leave them to rot and fall, they won't give flower and keep producing, as their natural cycle has been ignored. That would be madness. Imagine being able to say, when a friend drops by on a summer evening for a G 'n' T or Campari, 'I'll be with you in the picking of a lemon' – to paraphrase Oliver Goldsmith – before you rush out to the garden on your exotic errand. Then you bring in the glorious, fragrant fruit, with perhaps a glossy, elliptical leaf or two left seductively on the stalk.

The sub-tropical Meyer's Lemon is the most suitable for pot culture in our temperate climate, tolerating temperatures as low as 20 degrees Fahrenheit. Like children and dogs, fruit trees in pots love to spend as much time as possible out in the sunshine and fresh air for good health and compact growth. But at the first sign of real cold, your lemon will have to go indoors for the winter. An unheated greenhouse or conservatory is best, as it gets no resting period with heat and can become stringy and lose its leaves.

It's such a relief to know that when I use the zest of my new lemons I won't be ingesting a load of chemical garbage along with the essential oil. Using the zest and peel of commercial citrus fruits always made me uneasy before this. So I'm going to look after it very well, buy it a beautiful new pot and give it fresh, ericaceous compost, with some loam added for weight and its water-retaining properties, as it should never dry out completely. Good drainage is essential – the roots could easily rot if left in stagnant water – so a good inch of crocks covered by a layer of well-rotted manure or moist peat will go in first. It likes a high-nitrogen, medium-potassium feed, little and often.

Potted-up trees can live in the same pot for the rest of their long lives. Those in large containers should have the top two inches of compost scraped away every spring and replaced with a fresh mixture. When they go outside, give them the sunniest spot you can find out of strong winds, either standing decoratively on a level surface or plunged to the rim of their pots into the ground, which saves on watering. Propagation is by layering or summer cuttings, though the Meyer's, uniquely, will produce fruit from pips. So me and my lemon are going to have lots of very pretty offspring sometime in the future, most of which I'll probably have to give up for adoption.

Cherries

From June to August life could be just a bowl of cherries, but in Ireland it rarely is. The best of the ornamental cherries, their fleeting time of beauty more than welcome in their season, are another subject altogether. But the sight of a bowl of sweet, fresh, shiny and plump cherry fruits piled pretty and high is a rare one in an Irish house. To buy the imported ones in any decently decadent quantity costs a small fortune – about £5 a pound for a bag which doesn't last bathtime. Irish cherries are as rare as hen's teeth on the market, maybe because the people who do grow them here can't resist eating them all themselves.

Cherry trees are handsome, with large serrated dark leaves giving good autumn colour. In many cases the bark is decorative too, ringed with rich brown or silver patches. Cherry blossom in spring is magnificent, surpassing in beauty all but the choicest ornamental Prunus. In the days before they started to chop them all down, people in England made an annual pilgrimage to Kent each spring to see the miles of cherry orchards in full, delicate blossom. The soil in commercial cherry country is usually limey and chalky, alkaline. But it is easy to create the right conditions in the average Irish garden, while in Dublin in particular the right conditions already exist.

Cherries, both sweet and sour, are not too fussy, thriving in any deep, well-drained soil, preferably alkaline. Lime can be added, at four to eight ounces a square yard, if there's a deficiency. Their biggest enemies are an acid or waterlogged soil, frost pockets and birds, who will eat all the fruit if you don't net it in time.

This is one good reason for growing them trained against a wall; even grafted on a dwarfing rootstock, they are mighty big trees if left to grow as standards and this makes it difficult, if not impossible, to net them. They can be trained as fans, festoons or espaliers on south or west walls, while the later-fruiting sour cherries like the self-fertile Morello – good for pies, jams, bottling and liquor (Kirsch, cherry brandy), or dessert if left to go black – will grow, blossom and fruit on any wall, even a dour north wall. They can be grown in pots in the back yard where space is limited.

With the exception of the North American variety, 'Stella', sweet cherries are self-sterile and need a pollinator. The acid cherries – another good variety is Kentish Red which ripens in July – are suitable pollinators for some, and sweet varieties from one group will do the job for those in another group. A reliable fruit grower should be able to guide you on this.

Autumn is the time to start thinking about planting this ancient fruit, known to have been cultivated by the Mesopotamians. Dig the planting hole deep and wide, at least one and a half times the width of the rootball, and spread out the roots horizontally, taking care not to damage the bark, which protects the tree by barring the way to unwelcome diseases. Work in plenty of compost or old leaves, but not manure – cherries are vigorous and don't need that kind of encouragement. Even on naturally alkaline soils, add lime (or old limestone rubble if you can find it) at planting time, and every third or fourth winter after that.

Like other fruits, they need potash; an annual mulch of garden compost, or ashes straight from a wood fire, will satisfy their needs. They are shallow-rooting, posing no threat to wall foundations, but their roots do need some protection. Soak wall-planted trees weekly when they're fruiting. At cherry-picking time, allow the fruit to stay on the tree as long as possible – the longer they stay, the sweeter they become – but catch them before they split.

It is best to cut them off with stalk intact using a scissors, but take care not to include the twig, as this could create an entry point for bacterial canker and silverleaf, diseases to which they are prone. If there is a very severe frost they may need some winter protection, but in most parts of Ireland this danger can be avoided by planting them in a sheltered spot that is not a frost-pocket.

Acid cherries fruit on growth made the previous year, not on older wood. Autumn is the best time to cut away old stems, back to a sturdy new shoot, which you tie in to replace them. Sweet cherries, on the other hand, fruit on spurs that form along the entire length of the two-year-old wood and wall-trained specimens are pruned in summer and again in autumn, no later than September.

The mysteries of fruit pruning are best learned when there is an accompanying diagram or visual aid, or by watching an experienced person do it; for example, Finola Reid is a good teacher, making it look logical, which it is, on her television slot. Please don't let something like pruning put you off growing cherries. Buy a good book on the subject if you don't have someone to show you, and every summer will be a big bowl of cherries.

Wild Plants of Dublin

There were so many derelict sites in Dublin before the current building boom that it was easy to guess the species of flora that would col-
onize the capital should it be allowed fall into total decay. Some of
them, such as the hart's tongue fern, the common red poppy, purple
foxgloves and blue speedwell – once sewn onto clothes in Ireland to
safeguard travellers – are native.

Others have been around so long that we take it for granted
they're native. But such familiar things as wall valerian, fuchsia, rose-
bay willow herb, montbretia, ivy-leaved toad flax and even the ubiquitous sycamore (*Acer pseudoplatanus*), are in fact introductions,
garden escapees. Another colonizer we've all grown used to is
Buddleia davidii, the Butterfly Bush. First found by a French missionary on the Tibetan–Chinese border as late as 1869, it was only
introduced to these islands at the turn of the century.

Now that buddleia (also spelt buddleja) has become more Irish
than the Irish themselves, most people have encountered it *in urbis*.
It's sometimes confused with lilac (*Syringa*), which flowers in May
and is quite a different plant. It has long, mauve, sometimes purple
or even white flower spikes from July to October and flourishes on
stony waste ground, which is a good substitute for its shingly mountain home in Tibet and China. Winged and light, its seeds can travel
a fair distance on the wind, enabling them to establish themselves
readily in any old cracked chimney or neglected masonry. The flowers smell strongly of honey and buddleia bushes can be literally covered with bees and moths when in bloom.

About ten years ago, tomatoes began to appear in Dublin, growing out of cracked sewage pipes on the walls of old houses and causing great excitement. The media got interested and as a result, everybody now knows that tomato seeds pass undigested through the

human system. Bush tomatoes of the French variety are a weed in the warmer parts of France. Over there, once you have planted them, you have cherry tomatoes for life. In my last garden, much nearer the city centre and very sheltered, they reappeared three years running and gave some fruit. It makes me think it should be possible to have a permanent cherry tomato patch here, if some winter shelter were given.

A marvellous self-seeding event has happened in a front garden on the main road near here. It began a few years ago, when a woman moved in and started gardening in a slightly haphazard way. She was lavish in her planting, and an eclectic but mostly good mix of things began to appear in the first summer. Then the garden was abandoned to its own devices, with paper sacks of real manure left lying around for months until they leached away into the borders.

This year her garden has already been a near riot of foxgloves, aconitum, blue geraniums and other earlies, but right now it is a sea of tall, upright evening primrose (*Oenothera*) foliage waiting to explode into a canvas of sunny yellow. It has become a talking point among the regulars at the bus stop outside her wall, who are watching developments. They won't be disappointed. Over in Sligo, too, it has seeded itself unexpectedly in the gaps in an experienced gardener's big, new border. She is delighted with the way it has placed itself.

We've already seen the tall Himalayan balsam, *Impatiens glandulifera*, aggressively take its place among its peers in the wilder areas outside towns, particularly in the warmer coastal areas. Now it's hit Dublin and because it holds itself upright and is quite decorative, with masses of pale pink to claret flowers on thick red stems and large, coarsely elegant dark green leaves, it has been welcomed as a friend to the floras of the city's wastelands. But it does need watching, being capable of casting its seeds for a dozen yards in every direction, and is something of a mixed blessing in the garden.

Not so the Great Mullein, *Verbascum thapsus*, variously known as Jesus' Flannel and Our Lady's Candle because of its great downy grey leaves and tapering spires of yellow flowers. It suddenly appears from nowhere, though it hasn't shown up here yet. I am pleased this year with a tall, sturdy white verbascum (barely tinged with pink on two of its upper petals) that has hybridized itself here from a mixture of two cultivated types – a Cotswold Queen and a smaller, unnamed variety.

Another exotic that has recently taken to the streets is the big *Geranium palmatum*, an evergreen four-footer similar to *G. maderense*, with good foliage and rather sticky pink flowers. In my garden it has taken to the high ground and seeded itself in a broken part of the stone wall, effectively outshining the pesky valerian.

The tall purple toad flax, *Linaria purpurea*, a perennial originally brought over from Italy, has been falling on stony ground and graciously doing its bit to fill the city's derelict sites. The yellow Welsh poppy, *Meconopsis cambricans*, is always welcome for a while in spring. It too is prone to feckless seeding and has to be dug out if it grows where it's not wanted. Its roots go deep and are very stubborn. If you remove the seed heads while they are still green – a tedious job – it can be kept in its place. But much better to catch the pods when they're ripe, carry them around in your pocket until you find a bit of bare waste ground that needs cheering up and scatter them. Like all poppy seed, they can take a time to get started, so you may have to wait a couple of years to admire the results of your guerrilla tactic.

Roll on the day when the still uncommon Mexican daisy, *Erigeron karvinskianus*, gets over the garden walls and makes a name for itself in the wilder reaches of the city. As a colonizer *manqué* it's had plenty of practice, being quite expert at seeding itself prettily in stone walls and under steps. But it would want to hurry, if it's to stay ahead of the Celtic Tiger, or its seed will fall and waste on hard new ground, the concrete layer spreading over the loose stone of the old city.

Ivy

One of the most arresting winter sights in this neighbourhood is an ordinary wall, with tall entrance pillars leading to a quiet cul-de-sac, which has been utterly transformed into an object of great beauty by swoops, loops and swags of the common ivy, *Hedera helix*, now in full flower. But despite its unassuming beauty and usefulness in the garden, the poor Hedera family has got itself a bad name, a reputation as a great destroyer.

People are afraid of it, even when it's confined to a pot and used as a house-plant, which you can do with all ivies. As a result, the hederas in all their wonderful variety are not seen nearly as often as they deserve, in either private or public planting schemes. All over Ireland there are eyesores crying out to be laced with ivy, a multi-purpose stalwart of the bleak winter garden and one of the most beautiful evergreen climbers we can grow in our temperate northern climate.

Even the experts have failed to agree. Opinion on the subject is sharply divided between those who think it's a good and noble plant and those who rail at its murderous habit of killing trees, destroying masonry and getting in under the eaves of the roof to lift slates and tiles. Risteard Mulcahy, the erstwhile heart surgeon, in his influential and keenly observed little book *For the Love of Trees* (1996), points out that the effect of ivy on the well-being of trees has never been subjected to proper scientific analysis. Without such an enquiry, he argues, a balanced judgment cannot be reached. 'Whatever about its possible deleterious effect, ivy will remain a common and traditional feature of our environment,' he writes. 'But if its excessive growth does do damage to trees, hedgerows and other structures, it should be subjected to proper control.'

And there you have it, the answer to the ivy question: control – and choosing the right variety for the right place, whether woody-stemmed, trailing or clinging, so that it never gets seriously out of hand in the first place. I know the terrors of ivy, having spent long days trying to rescue old apple trees in a neglected Donegal orchard from its suffocating embrace. The stems were twisted into weird and wonderful shapes, as thick as a child's torso in places and tough as iron.

Obviously you're not going to allow this happen at home. If you see the vigorous green type has seeded itself in an unwanted place, dig it out while it is still small and harmless. As for destroying walls, if the pointing is sound it won't do any damage. A self-clinger like ivy is a nuisance on a wall that has to be repainted at decent intervals, but otherwise it does an extraordinarily good job of keeping the wall insulated and dry. However, ivy will eventually dislodge loose mortar and do damage to paintwork, so be warned.

Where an existing, vigorous ivy is trying to get under the roof of a building (and this is a bad habit shared by wistarias, *Clematis montana* and the climbing hydrangea, *H. petiolaris*), either cut it hard back to the wall face or chop right down to a few feet and let it start again. Young leaf growth on ivies is by the far the prettiest.

Before you choose an ivy from the huge range on offer, think carefully about where you want to place it and find out all about its habits and eventual height. They range in height from ground-huggers, to tree-climbers reaching thirty feet or more. Except for the few slightly tender species, mostly from North Africa, the Canaries and Madeira, which need a very sheltered wall or even indoor conditions, most ivies, and all of the *H. helix* types, are fully hardy.

In general, I don't like the big-leaved fellows, though they have their place. *H. canariensis*, '*Gloire de Marengo*' *variegata,* is good, with an irregular mixture of white ivory, pale grey-green and darker green leaves. As for the very popular *H. dentata* 'Sulphur Heart', syn. 'Paddy's Pride', I find it slightly nauseating, even though it carries the RHS seal of approval. Its leaves are just too big, floppy, shapeless and coarse, and its colour is a bilious combination of sulphurous yellow and pale green. The little ones, such as the prettily variegated 'Glacier' (only grows to six feet and looks particularly good with white flowers), 'Buttercup' (the young foliage is a warm, soft buttery yellow), the fine-leaved *H. helixpedata* 'Caenwoodiana', the tiny 'Adam' and 'Silver Queen' – all these are much easier to place, decorative in winter and amenable to regular snipping.

Ivies come in all shapes, sizes and colours, including some tipped with purples and reds and upright growers (*H. congesta, H. erecta*). The very decorative ones deserve to be planted as a feature in their own right, and not just to mask an eyesore. One of the best ways to use it in a small garden, where space cannot be found for a columnar Irish yew or some other strong, evergreen feature, is to train it on an upright structure, such as a pyramid, pergola or arch, where it will look good all year round but absolutely fantastic in winter.

Whether used as a fast-growing evergreen backdrop up which other climbers can scramble in their season, or for frilling the edges of tubs planted with spring bulbs, or decorating the mantelpiece and dinner table at Christmas, the much-maligned ivies are your only man. And just in case you're still not convinced of its worth, ivies grown as house-plants clean the air of harmful benzene, while their cousins outdoors provide the birds with generous quantities of berries to help them through the long, hard winters.

GREAT IRISH GARDENS

Kilfane

When Nicholas and Susan Mosse first arrived at Kilfane about ten years ago, the place had been taken over by rhododendrons. Mauve *Rhododendron ponticum*, the one you see marching across mountains all over Ireland, had been planted when new and fashionable two hundred years before and had gone completely wild. It pushed hard against the windows, trying to get in, followed closely by an army of laurel. Dead timber was thick underfoot and even the trees were stalking out of the woods towards the former gamekeeper's lodge and dower house, then cowering on its forty acres of wilderness near Thomastown, Co. Kilkenny.

Spongeware potter Nicholas and his American wife Susan, a Renaissance woman of ideas and action, started to clear it all away, urged on by their friend Sue Finlay, a garden consultant from Scotland who would come over regularly and say: 'Keep taking it away, keep clearing. Go for it.' They kept going through the forty acres of overgrown woodland that came with it, all the way down to the deep, dark ravine with its stream rushing over mysterious black rocks on its way to the river Nore.

As they cleared, releasing oak, birch and beech into the light and planting ferns, dicentras, bluebells and *Anemone rivularis* underfoot, they reclaimed the house and the old walled orchard with its few remaining fruit trees. But it was not until the night of Hurricane Charlie, which devastated town and country alike, that the Mosses discovered the ravine's great secret.

The painter Barrie Cooke and sculptor Bill Woodrow were up in the house when Nicholas, who had been out inspecting the damage, came rushing in babbling incoherently about a waterfall. They all rushed down the steep slopes to the swollen river and witnessed a minor miracle. Cascading over the top of a forty-foot cliff, where Nick had often looked and wished for a waterfall, was a veritable cataract. The lads immediately jumped in and frolicked about in the deep pool that had formed at its base – and there it has ruled ever since.

Following the course of the fall along a man-made canal for over a mile, the Mosses found a head race where the river had been diverted. On the floor of the ravine, facing the new discovery, the bones of a house had always puzzled them. Intrepid architect Jeremy Williams took himself off and found Ordnance Survey maps from the 1830s. Very faint and barely legible was a thatched 'cottage *orné*' or summer house, a grassed and planted glade, a hermit's grotto and, of course, the fall. These treasures dated from the early 1790s and the Mosses realized they had a jewel from the Romantic Age on their hands.

The two-storey cottage, with its dalliance parlour and ornate straw thatch, is now faithfully recreated. Every detail, from the locally quarried cobbles, hazel and vine furniture made by the gardener, Pat Butler, to the roses, clematis, honeysuckle and jasmine around the doors and windows, is in period. A tea-house for the public now, it may soon be available for 'second honeymoons, a writer's retreat, or interesting weekends', according to Nick, who says it's very difficult bringing the milk and tea down every day.

It is a full two miles from Kilfane House, where the landowning Power family who built it once lived. The only access was on foot, and old documents tell of cold supper parties given there for up to twenty people. Found too were letters singing the praises of its rarefied air (it's ionized by the rushing water and does make you feel good) and sweetly melancholic aspect. The grotto, with original steps leading to the top of the waterfall, is to be restored with the help of a grant from the Heritage Council.

In the upper gardens at Kilfane there is much to see. Spaces are being made with art in mind. Already there is James Tyrrell's *Air Mass*, Bill Woodrow's impressive *Rut* and a crazy acrylic distorting mirror by Sean Mulcahy which catches you unawares along a fern and laurel walk and literally deconstructs you as you move towards it. Great fun. Gardening doyen Jim Reynolds helped Susan plan and plant, and the pool garden, with its dining pergola and cut granite salvaged from the old platforms at Kilkenny railway station, is deeply pleasant.

You step down from this, past twin stone troughs filled with the heavily scented dianthus, 'Mrs Sinkins', into what Susan calls her Moon Garden. In a formal layout around a central circle are informally planted beds, overflowing with the best of white and silver perennials set off by smoky purple foliage – 'Chiaroscuro', says Susan. Seasonal gaps are filled with annual nicotiana and cosmos, raised from seed in the private kitchen garden behind the house.

Kilfane is a work in progress, having opened to the public much sooner than its owners intended when an EU cultural grant came through. A frog pond, planted with *Iris setosa*, arums, white foxgloves and primulas, greets you at the public entrance. It is located two miles from Thomastown in the foothills of Graiguenamanagh. Phone 056-24558 for a private appointment or to order a delicious picnic basket in advance, complete with Nicholas Mosse pottery.

Beech Park

In the 1960s and '70s, when I was growing up on the north side of Dublin, the city was dotted with farms and green fields. The cattle market and abbatoir were on the North Circular Road. Cows, sheep and even donkeys would run down our road and into our gardens on market days and their manure would be shovelled up by on-the-ball gardeners like my father. Many of the animals came from local farms, which stretched out past Oxmantown and the Phoenix Park, past the villages ringing the city, past the Guinness estates and into deepest Clonsilla.

Dubliners took this healthy blend of town and country for granted. They didn't seem to notice when their birthright to fresh air and natural landscape was gradually eroded through bad planning and development. Suddenly, by the late 1980s, it was open season on every little green space. Money was made hand over fist by those in the front line. Beautiful buildings came tumbling down and endless ribbons of production-line houses filled up the fields between the villages and hamlets.

Some years ago, on my first visit to the Shackletons' garden, Beech Park, in Clonsilla, I sensed that something of the essential character of Dublin had been preserved after all. Here, a few miles from town on a corner of the Liffey valley, was timeless beauty, a two-hundred-year-old private treasure open to the nation for the price of a pint. A walk of beech trees led past a tiny gate lodge and grazing cattle. The Regency house, clad in bleached terracotta, was in need of repair after a big fire. A wildflower meadow and an arboretum brought me through an arch into a cobbled yard, where white doves flew from cote to clock and geese rent the air with their clackety conversations.

Homemade stalls, lined with rare and fantastic plants from the two-acre walled garden beyond, were for sale on one side. A tack-room warmed by a wood-burning stove lit up another, offering warmth, tea, coffee, scones with jam, chocolate cake. I couldn't believe it. This place was completely alive and organic, lived in and cared for by one family of scientists and gardeners for nearly two hundred years. And as a bonus, the gardeners and custodians of Beech Park, Jonathan Shackleton and Daphne Levinge, were on hand, like good tutors, to teach me from their vast store of plant knowledge.

One of the best things about Beech Park, besides its unparalleled plant collection, was its naturalness. Here they knew that nature is an ally, not something to be rigidly tamed and controlled: it's always there beyond the walls, and it's never quite banished from the garden itself. The borders were made with a lavish generosity, giving things plenty of elbow room. Plants were labelled discreetly on metal tags, helping the student. It was an inspiration. Noted modern gardeners, like Rachel Lambe, are deeply grateful for their apprentice year in the Shackleton potting sheds.

This irreplaceable piece of Dublin is lost to us after today, the last open day before the house and garden change hands next month. Forced to sell, the Shackletons gave first offer to the State. The State professed itself dead keen to buy, but for some reason, which was never satisfactorily explained, didn't make a serious bid. The gardens, and sixty-four acres of prime west Dublin land, were sold instead to an auctioneer-farmer for just over £700,000. His plans for the garden are unclear, although he has, reportedly, already engaged a gardener.

Meanwhile, the Shackletons are taking cuttings and divisions of most of the plants, heeling them in temporarily in friends' gardens, hoping they will survive the year before being moved to their new permanent home in County Cavan. No doubt they will embrace the challenge and make another wonderful garden, from scratch this time. But two hundred years of history, love and dedication to plant life were there at Beech Park, for everyone to benefit from, and now we've lost it.

In the last weeks the garden has put on a brave show, looking lovely, but sad. It's not just the dying year that's lending it such a forlorn air. It's as if the plants know they are being left behind to face an uncertain future. Will the garden just disappear like a lost city in the jungle? Is that what happens to great gardens in modern, EU-funded Ireland?

But I still have the many plants I bought there, which I will carefully divide and share out as they increase over time. And memories, of course. Selfishly, I admit, some of my fondest are of rainy, end-of-season afternoons, when hardly anyone else turned up and you could wander around the borders in splendid isolation, stealing one last look at old friends among the plants before they died back for the coming winter, before taking refuge from the cold and damp by the stove, sipping tea and watching the family dogs mooch around the courtyard in the fading autumn light.

Cluain na dTor

Not many people know this, but if you happen to be in the north-west of Ireland, it pays to read the ads printed on the side of cartons of *bainne úr* from Donegal Creameries. This is how I discovered the appropriately named Cluain na dTor, the Meadow of Shrubs, which happens to be the only nursery in the north-west specializing in sea-side plants.

In a heavily populated county exposed to sea winds at nearly every bend in the road, it would seem astonishing that Seamus O'Donnell's budding nursery is the only one specializing, until he reminds you that, for historical reasons, there is not much tradition of gardening in Donegal beyond vegetable, fruit and hydrangea-growing – outside the big estates, such as nearby Glenveagh Castle, Dunlewy and Bally-connell House, the last just down the road from him outside Falcarragh.

This is changing very, very slowly and one of those at the forefront of this change is Seamus O'Donnell, a man with a mission. After studying botanical science, which he says 'only teaches you about trees and flowers, not plants as such,' he went travelling. In this he was emulating his grandfather, who sailed to Alaska at the beginning of the century to work on the Klondike, coming back with the means to build the fine house and outbuildings, on about four acres of land beside the sea, that are now home to the nursery, Seamus himself and his partner, Deirdre Ní Bhraonain, herself an artist, ace vegetable grower and bodhrán-playing member of the musical family that gave the world Clannad and Enya.

When Seamus's travels took him to Australia, his original mission – 'to create wildlife habitats all around the country, plant hedging where birds can nest, trees for shelter, and in some way contribute to the environment' – opened up into a fascination with southern-hemisphere plants and the possibilities for growing them in his native Donegal. Soon he cast his keen plantsman's eye on the other countries in the southern hemisphere noted for their fabulous flora and sympathetic climates. New Zealand, Tasmania, Chile – which he believes 'hasn't been fully explored yet in relation to Ireland' – and South Africa all came in for study and experiment.

He was now living at Cluain na dTor and winning back the ground foot by overgrown foot. He did a Shannon Development course in starting your own agri-business and played drums in a band for which Deirdre played keyboards. All the time he was making forays in search of plants to the nearest seaside nursery, in Clifden, Connemara, and bringing them home and propagating them. Seven years ago he opened a nursery which sold only bare-root plants and started a landscaping service.

Now he has help and most of his stock can also be bought potted. He has a good supply of herbaceous perennials for sale: big, strong healthy ones bursting out of their pots, enough in most of them to divide and multiply immediately, and all at a fair price. He is nursing a collection of more than fifty hebes, though many of them 'are still wee', like the many different microclimates he is creating by planting hundreds of trees and shrubs every winter.

He has a range of olearias, hedging, trees and shrubs, including *Ozothamnus*, Tenerife Broom, which flowers outside for him in a mild winter, *Fascicularia bicolor* growing in shade, though it is recommended only for the warmest counties, Correas, Corokias, Liptospermum thriving in a spot blasted by south-westerly winds, and the desirable conifer *Podocarpussalignus*, with soft, pendulous, almost tropical dark-green foliage.

Away from the public area, where he is making a specimen garden with lots of stone, sculptures, secret corners and seats for contemplation, is the private potting and hardening-off area, Deirdre's impressive vegetable garden guarded by the skeleton of a washed-up whale, a lean-to greenhouse where tomatoes shoot up the walls fed only on homemade comfrey fertilizer, and an enormous plastic tunnel crammed with cuttings, ranging from the humble Forsythia to an array of *Phormium tenax*, a striking display of coloured grasses (another plant he wants to experiment with in the landscaped environment), and the pretty-leaved *Pseudowintera colorata* from New Zealand, a slow grower to about nine feet, which keeps its colour in shade.

When he has brought on southern-hemisphere plants in the tunnel, they are tested for hardiness outside in nursery beds. If a plant proves hardy, only then will he recommend it. His mission now is spreading the word, turning Donegal on to the life-enhancing qualities of beautiful plants. But it is a lonely business at times, and occasionally he has seen people from his area buying unsuitable plants in nurseries in faraway towns. Until recently, when he met Seán Ó Gaothín, the head gardener at Glenveagh, he says he knew no other gardener to discuss plants with at all, except for his mother, who, he explains, has always had the gift of growing things wisely and well.

Ozothamnus

Ardgillan Castle

'You'll find me in the herbaceous border,' was the arrangement made by Dominica McKenna, the young gardener at Ardgillan Castle, near Balbriggan in north County Dublin. For the past four years she has been transforming the place, aided by two permanent general workers, a man who cuts the grass and, recently, a diligent student gardener from the Botanic Gardens in Glasnevin.

Ardgillan demesne, on about two hundred acres of parkland sweeping down to the Irish Sea, was bought by Dublin County Council – now Fingal – in 1981, as part of their policy of maintaining the county's material heritage and creating a ring of public parks for the people's pleasure around the city's suburbs. The former home of the Taylour family, who came to Ireland from Sussex in 1653 to do the first ordnance survey so that Cromwell could work out who to plant where, Ardgillan has been described as the undiscovered jewel in the crown of the north side. The first sudden sight of it, from the brow of a hill as you drive in, will take your breath away.

The eye rests first on a castellated Georgian country house of pale stone nestling in a wide, elegant sweep behind a line of stately yews at the bottom of the hill, then moves beyond to feast on a panoramic view of the glittering sea, islands and mountains. From this elevated piece of coastline you can see the Cooley peninsula and the Mourne mountains beyond, and Lambay Island lying off the coast. The long stretch of once-private beach on the far side of the Dublin–Belfast railway line is reached by a footbridge known as the Lady's Stairs, said to be haunted by the ghost of Edith Shackleton, who drowned at sea.

But on to the garden as arranged. There was Dominica, a native of north Louth, Felco secateurs holstered and ready at the hip as she worked her way through the tall, rain-swept plants at the back of the long border, still full of colour but going over now at the end of

August. After taking a diploma in commercial horticulture at the ICA's An Grianán in Warrenstown, her first job was a six-month winter stint for Westmeath County Council, planting the wasteland verges on the Athlone bypass.

That year, 1992, the county council was taking on new gardeners – 'and I got this', she says, waving her strong and capable hands around her demesne. 'It was a wilderness then,' a fact she illustrated with photographs. Besides the yews, some mature woodland that she's now planting in the faux-wild style of William Robinson, the formal rose garden started in '87 and a handsome *Cordyline australis*, standing solo in the two-and-three-quarter-acre walled garden, all was utter dereliction.

The garden proper starts when you go through a wide opening in the newish but already formidable hedge of Leyland cypresses, planted as a windbreak for a new beech hedge around the rose garden. The Leylandiis have plenty of space and can look smart enough if clipped regularly, though never as smart as yews. On the right is a wonderfully symmetrical nineteenth-century glasshouse, made of wood at the wings and curvilinear metal at its high, domed centre. Removed from the Jameson house at Seamount in Malahide and believed to be a replica of the one at Balmoral, it was faithfully reconstructed by council staff down to the original staging and curved-glass roof tiles, which ingeniously direct rainwater into the gutters. The run-off is then carried by pipes into big lead tanks for use inside.

When it rains, Dominica can be found here nursing a growing collection of interesting specimens, or in the castle itself making labels and cataloguing each and every plant. Otherwise she swims, but 'never sits', and says that from the age of about nine she knew quite clearly that she wanted to make gardening her life. Both her mother and grandmother were good gardeners and when she's home at week-ends she gardens there.

The stone-walled garden is broken up into a series of themed smaller gardens, beginning with the Four Seasons one, which she admits 'has a long way to go'. Pass on into a flower garden of some interest which holds the original old Cordyline. Next is an Irish Garden in the making, which she is filling with plants discovered or bred by Irish women and men. There's the fruit garden, with the south wall prettily alcoved along its length and used for its original purpose of growing heat-loving peaches, kiwi, grapes, pears and nectarines.

The box-edged vegetable garden, its produce used by the castle restaurant's cooks, is beautiful in form and colour, as well as bountiful. Great squares of boxed-in corn make bold centrepieces along its length and adventurous planting of unusual varieties make it a place to linger. It's hard to believe that this was a wilderness when President Robinson offically opened the house and park a few years ago.

But the *pièce de résistance*, and Dominica's own favourite, is the lush, warm and fragrant herb garden, drowsy with the hum of bees and alive with marvellous butterflies. Perfect circles of box hedging, bay trees at their centre, run down its length. Other beds are square, rectangular or curved, each one containing a different set of herbs with different uses: medicinal, culinary, for potpourri and for dyeing. The walls are clothed in rare and not so rare shrubs and climbers. It was almost impossible to leave this paradise, with something new and sensuous at every turn.

Primrose Hill

A snowdrop is a snowdrop is a snowdrop, or is it? Well, I've just met my first galanthophile – a person bewitched, besotted but never bewildered by the elegant *Galanthus* (snowdrop) family – who introduced me to a dazzling array of different sorts growing at Primrose Hill, his family's six-acre garden on the edge of Lucan village in Co. Dublin.

'Most people think there are only two kinds of snowdrops, spring- and autumn-flowering, but there are hundreds of species and cultivars,' explained Robin Hall, whose grand passion was first ignited by reading Patrick Synge's *Collins Guide to Bulbs* in 1960 when he was a schoolboy. Though he will not claim the honour, his collection is acknowledged by the gardening cognoscenti as the best and most comprehensive in Ireland – by miles. He deserves to be designated as the holder of the National Snowdrop Collection.

Robin's mother Cicely started the present garden in 1957, when the family moved from Balbriggan to what was then a beautiful but run-down manse. The previous incumbent was a Scots Presbyterian minister, Dr Irwin, a close friend and confidant of President Eamon de Valera.

Once a stolid farmhouse of fairly ancient provenance, Primrose Hill was added to substantially in the late eighteenth or early nineteenth century, most probably by James Gandon, architect of the Custom House, who lived nearby for twenty years. Part of the house can be visited on open days and is included in the £3 admission fee. Guarded by stately Florence Court yews, the house is not very large but it is very beautiful. The front hall and stairs are exceptionally pretty and the lovely dining-room has an enormous, floor-length curved window which looks out over the unfolding tapestry of the garden. Primrose Hill is one of the few gardens to open for early spring bulbs, and in July and August it opens again, for the lilies, herbaceous lobelias and other interesting perennials, many of them unusual and some unique, having been bred there by a mixture of nature and design over the years.

Alongside Robin Hall's carefully placed drifts of different snow-drops, there are yellow pools of winter aconites (*Eranthis hyemalis*) nestling in rough grass along the beech-lined drive. In the shelter of the garden proper, there are great big patches of dark rose *Cyclamen coum*. The gorgeous blue *reticulata* Iris, *I. histroides*, the Juno and rare Baker irises, rare and wonderful primulas and celandines, are just a sample of what the keen plantsperson can see coming into flower in late January.

Cicely Hall is a deeply knowledgeable plantswoman who wears her scholarship lightly. Ask her something about a plant and imme-diately names, history, inspiration and expert advice are delivered in a witty and entertaining way. Not being a total galanthophile like her son, who confesses to seeing all other plants as just 'filling for the snowdrops, an orchestra surrounding the main event', she has amassed a fascinating collection of Irish perennials during the forty years she has been gardening at Primrose Hill. Some which find shel-ter there are the nearly extinct (in Ireland) perennial wallflower Miss Massey, and the old double Harpur Crewe.

Learning about the different snowdrops from Robin Hall is a rev-elation. When he kneels down in front of them and tenderly lifts their pendent heads, stroking back a tepal to reveal their distinctly different markings, his involvement is complete. He reels off their names: Sam Arnott from Scotland; the famous Straffan, with two flowers, which was brought to Ireland by soldiers returning from the Crimea; two Primrose Hill Specials; the double Irish cultivar Hill Poe; Merlin; *Gracilus*, *Reginae-olgae*, which can flower as early as October; *Nivalis poculiformis*, a freak.

There are zillions more, but he won't commit himself to a specific number, not least because he doesn't want to appear boastful. He works tirelessly on behalf of his large family, fussing after them, dress-ing them with sieved leafmould, dividing and multiplying them with 'just a little pinch of bonemeal and river sand; I wouldn't feel comfortable using strong chemicals', and carefully planning the direction of the next drift, the new courses he will devise for his undulating rivers and clumps of pure white.

Because the garden at Primrose Hill is on an esker of sand and gravel, the drainage is sharp – not ideal for snowdrops, which like things wet in winter. The day I was there Robin was praying for rain to bring them on in time for the opening. To lose the common, ultra-tough snowdrop, *G. nivalis*, seems impossible but the hybrids, some costing as much as £20 for a single bulb, are a riskier affair. If subjected to botrytis, or severe drought or neglect, they can just fade away and disappear completely, never to be seen again.

When you go to Primrose Hill, don't expect manicured lawns, cream teas, or knicky-knacky seats and arbours. The Halls say their garden is a mixture of benign neglect and intense cultivation and most definitely the plants come first. Luckily, some of these are potted up for sale to visitors. Robin spends a whole month potting, and the result is pots bursting with healthy specimens.

Primrose Hill is not really suitable for frisky young children and access is limited for people in wheelchairs. To get there from Dublin, leave the motorway and go through the centre of Lucan. Immediately past the Garda station, on the same side, is a narrow turn, Primrose Lane. Leave your car in the lane and walk. The entrance gate is black and just past two very old cottages on the left. The phone number is 01 6280373.

Ardcarrig

For a long time now I've been a fan of Lorna MacMahon through her monthy West of Ireland notebook in *The Irish Garden* magazine. In her column, she engages the reader's interest with vivid, deeply knowledgeable accounts of her gardening experiences, the trials and triumphs met with as she works her way through almost five acres of rough and rocky land situated ten minutes out of Galway on the Moycullen road, near the shores of Lough Corrib.

When I heard that she worked absolutely alone to reclaim the land and make an intriguing series of gardens – the only work done by anyone else has been some professional rock-blasting – she assumed heroic stature. With her bare hands this tall, slender, agile woman has played god with the landscape, diverting rivers and streams to flow where she wants them to go, making pools, moving rocks and trees, building bridges and clearing impossibly wild places to make areas of rest, repose and intriguing planting.

About twenty-six years ago Lorna, her doctor husband Harry and their young sons moved to Ardcarrig at Oranswell, where they finally put down roots. Since their marriage they had moved nine times and no matter how small the space, in each one Lorna gardened. 'My first patch was small and I started with tomatoes. They were amazing, the most wonderful success. I was so full of myself and feeling so clever that there was no stopping me.'

When she finally realized her advantage – that she was blessed with ground used two years before as a hen-run and therefore fertilized to perfection for the growing of champion tomatoes – it was too late. Gardening had seeped into her bones and a plantswoman and gardener of near mythical proportions was loosed upon the world.

At the local hospital, Lorna works with psychiatric patients on plant-oriented therapy. While Ardcarrig is not open to the public at large, except for groups if arranged by phoning in advance, once a year she does host an open day in aid of the Galway Mental Health Association, a day that has become one of the highlights of the horticultural calendar. The proceeds help pay for those people coming out of psychiatric care into half-way houses.

So camouflaged by plant life is the exterior of the house (circa 1969) at Ardcarrig, that I found myself standing on its front step admiring the glossy new growth on a *Clematis armandii* before realizing with a slight shock that there was a house at all. Rather than the garden bowing to the house, *à la* the cardinal rule, it comes right up and embraces it.

The soil here is naturally poor and acid and full of honey fungus (*Armillaria mellia*), indigenous in the hazel wood now thickly carpeted with the bluebells which follow on from the wood anemones. The annual rainfall is sixty inches and the prevailing winds from the Atlantic are west and south-west. Over the years countless tons of improving horse manure and mushroom compost have been barrowed down to the gardens by Lorna. 'I've been lucky because horse manure is not rated around here, so I get as much as I can carry for free.'

There are already fourteen different sections with distinct personalities in Lorna's garden, including a Japanese area that boasts an impressive and authentic *uki-mi-doro* or snow-viewing lantern made of granite, which she says is an awesome sight at night when covered in snow with a lamp lit at its centre. But Lorna MacMahon is not finished yet (as if a garden could ever be finished), and is busy working on another two areas, on bits of land recently acquired from her friendly farming neighbour. One is a memorial garden, for which she has moved great trunks and roots of trees to expose powerful, angular slabs of granite.

She has used a crowbar to lever out rocks and got streams to run hither and thither and into interconnecting pools. A tapestry of shrubs will lead away from this garden for a loved one, until it ends with a row of cultivated gorse at the boundary where garden meets field, a field full of the wild gorse that takes the eye out over the grasses that line up along the edge of the waters of the heaving lake.

Ballinlough and Butterstream

In June 1997 I joined a bunch of people from the Garden & Landscape Designers Association for a tour of three gardens, which included a sneak preview of Ballinlough Castle in Westmeath and a guided tour of Butterstream near Trim, given by Jim Reynolds in top form. Ballinlough is the first recipient of EU money under the Great Gardens of Ireland Restoration Scheme. Because it looks like being such a good garden, it is worth getting to know it while it's young and following its progress as it grows up.

There are acres of intriguing old walled gardens which have been lying idle for years, with little known about their use before 1938, when the owners moved back from England during the war. In some places, shadows on the pale walls mark the spot where trained fruit trees grew long ago. The ground pitches in a queerly pleasant way and slopes take you by surprise, some of them falling by as much as three metres. Because the walls were allowed to follow the lively contours of the landscape, there are no right angles at all. I loved it.

Most of the work has been concentrated here within the walls and down by the stream, where a blue, white and yellow water garden is being planted. Back within the enclosures, a wisteria wall has been started and a large, still rectangular pool spreads calm where before there was an uptight 1940s red-brick pit, known as the sunken garden.

In the kitchen garden, an alcoholic hedge is planned – sloes for gin, elder for cordial and champagne, nuts for nibbling. A house needs flowers, and this is a fairly big house, so a picking garden is a certainty. A highly ornamental, octagonal fruit cage will be built, probably in the Gothic style, like the existing old doorways. Lovely, old-fashioned medlars, a fruit you should eat only when they are almost rotten, have pride of place in the newly stocked orchard.

Elsewhere, masses of French lavender edging and rich plantings of old roses and good herbaceous stuff are beginning to show their strength.

Ballinlough is set on 580 acres surrounding a beautiful famine lake, complete with island and a new but settled-looking wooden bridge, painted against the weather in the same navy blue as the castle's doors and windows. The lake curves around two sides of the soft grey house, which sits pretty as a picture on a hill, its feet lapped by wild silky meadow grasses.

We took tea in the house, though in the future there will be tea-rooms in the coachyard and the house will remain private. But there are beautiful views of it as you trek around the lake, where at least two kinds of wild orchid grow and dozens of badgers and foxes live. Since its core castle was first built in the sixteenth century, Ballinlough has been occupied by the O'Reillys, who changed their name at some strategic point in history from Ó Rathallaigh to Nugent – 'for money', said John Nugent when I asked why. They did not, however, change their Roman Catholic religion, which is probably why this big house outside the pale survived intact. Sir John and Pepe Nugent are the present incumbents and they are doing all the right things. 'We've come to gardening late in life,' said John. 'It was either God or Gardening and we chose Gardening.'

The follies, fun and fine plantsmanship of Jim Reynolds's mas-terpiece-in-progress, Butterstream Gardens on the outskirts of Trim, are admired not only by the masses but by the English monarch-in-waiting, Charlie Windsor, who has added Jim to the shortlist of high-powered consultants he retains to advise on his garden at Highgrove.

Jim Reynolds has been reclaiming fields from his father's farm over the past twenty years and has carved from them many mansions. At the centre of his garden, he has made a funny-serious sort of maze, a series of strongly structured little garden rooms all leading into and out of each other, with corridors running on either side like an old French country house built in the grand manner.

There is a lively, deep and well-planted stream running through it – the Butterstream. Its carefully planned surprises are best discovered for yourself. You can't miss them, there's one around every corner, more through the numerous arches and entrances clipped out of tall beech hedges which line the main paths. It is all cunningly orchestrated, and though you couldn't actually get lost, you could play a good party game of hide and seek.

At the end of June, there is always a lull in herbaceous planting when the strong colours of bulbs, peonies and Oriental poppies have retired for the year. Butterstream was no exception, with a quiet palette of whites, mauves, pinks, blues and some yellows repeated throughout most of the beds and borders, though in different configurations and against dramatically different backdrops.

In the rose parterre edged with box – 'grown high in the Italian style', according to Jim – the colour was lifted briefly by the fading beauty of old red Tuscany roses. The 'hot area', a small enclosure experimenting with structural foliage and strong yellows, reds and oranges, was still warming up for its July and August fling.

The voyage around Butterstream used to end in a generous, simple courtyard flanked on two sides by matching tea-houses, all built in the plain style of the early eighteenth century. Jim got a grant towards those. But now he is going ahead, off his own bat, on what must surely be the most ambitious private garden development happening in this country.

He is working on a staggering scale, to a grand plan along the lines of the Villa Lante in Italy. He is knee-deep in the process of turning a flat Meath field into a wide, grassed *allée* of lime trees stretching five hundred feet into the distance, and further into the borrowed view on the horizon. This walk will be mirrored on either side by two equally long, twenty-foot-wide canals which will end in a rushing cascade. These grand canals will, in turn, be flanked by two narrower lime walks, also stretching the full five hundred feet. The width of the finished 'garden room' will measure about a hundred feet. Jim Reynolds is mapping out his own personal landscape, and enjoying himself hugely.

Strokestown

Arriving ahead of the posse on the official opening day of the formal walled pleasure garden at Strokestown Park, I could feel the heat building up in layers, until it was thick and heavy, the air hot and damp from all the rain that had fallen in Co. Roscommon since St Swithin watered his own feast day on 15 July.

By mid-morning the Strokestown staff, a particularly amiable bunch of people, were saying it was to be the hottest day of the year. By noon the heat had wrapped itself around everything and was bending it to shape. There was no escaping it outdoors, even under the huge, rustling old copper beech in the walled garden. Cool was something only to be had indoors, inside the walls of the damp main house. Or, if the door was locked, as it is when a guided tour is in progress, there was always the cool interior of the stone-built famine museum, where the records showed that one of the tenants during that blighted time bore the name Callery, as in Jim Callery, the present owner of Strokestown, who famously bought it and much of its contents from the formidable Olive Pakenham Mahon in 1979.

There was another place into which you could duck to avoid the heat of the day, one with a much lower ceiling than any you would find in the big house, so uncomfortably low that even a medium-sized person like myself felt obliged to stoop when walking through it. This was the dank old servants' tunnel, connecting their living quarters to their places of work: the sculleries, cellars, kitchens and so on. The tunnel was built by a previous Pakenham so that he wouldn't ever have to mar his fantasy life with a sighting of one of the lower servants who made his privileged existence possible.

By 2.25 p.m., the time Fianna Fáil's Presidential wannabe, Roscommoner Albert Reynolds, stepped solo from a private company helicopter onto the rough lawn fronting the house, the fierce sun had pierced the mist and was busy burning up everything that moved. Looking dapper in a cool, light-coloured suit, Albert began by saying, 'You never lose anything by making a short speech.' His speech was very long, nonetheless. The melting crowd remained more or less good-humoured, until he quoted the official hand-out, saying the walled garden has gone into the Guinness Book of Records as having 'the longest herbaceous border in the British Isles'.

'British Isles?' rose the murmur. 'He of all people shouldn't call it that.' Talk turned to the garden. 'It was all brambles when I first saw it and the pond was like a bog,' said Galway gardener Lorna MacMahon. 'A jungle,' concurred architect Angela Jupe. Everybody agreed that Luke Dodd and Jim Reynolds were the seminal influences, the ones who had conceived the designs and plans for the restoration of the garden, laid out first as a cutting and vegetable garden when the house was built on the original O'Conor Roe land in the 1740s and later remodelled into a nineteenth-century pleasure ground.

Everybody also agreed that eminent gardeners Jonathan Shackleton, Daphne Levinge, Helen Dillon, Marcella Campbell and members of the Irish Garden Plant Society had given invaluable advice, ideas and plants ever since the garden restoration was mooted. But the well-sung heroes of the hour were undoubtedly the two women in pretty dresses, plantswoman-cum-designer Rachel Lamb and head gardener Caitriona White, who had laboured for years with FAS workers to bring the grand plan to fruition, adding their own ideas along the way.

Money was always a problem when doing the four-acre garden at Strokestown, despite financial support from the Heritage Council and the EU Regional Development Fund, but you'd never know it. When you first step onto the circle of cobbles inside the main gate the eye is drawn up a path lined on both sides by young Irish yews, leading to a pond flanked on its four corners by much older yews. Further on, the vista is further extended by a continuing yew walk until it ends in a folly, made from a Venetian window salvaged from the original eighteenth-century façade of the winged Palladian house.

On all sides there are young beeches waiting to grow up into enclosing walls. There is a baby maze, which apparently will be a doddle to get into when it grows, but a nightmare to get out of; the plan is to have concave distorting mirrors in the most unexpected places, adding to the confusion. In another part of the garden, geometric shapes in clipped yew will grow up and become a sound garden, with electronic cables activating odd sounds when trodden.

Some wonderful old trees, including two handsome tulip trees, a ginko, the copper beech and a stand of nut-producing hazels, grace the scene with their maturity. True to the spirit of the pleasure-garden principle, there is a formal rose garden, more follies and ornaments, a grass tennis court and a marvellously smooth croquet lawn. Other conceits include an alphabet walk in beech, a pergola in local stone and oak, a summer house, a fernery with woodland planting and a wildflower meadow.

All of these are in their infancy, waiting to grow up and take on substance. Right now the highlight is the truly magnificent, fantastically long herbaceous border with a sizzlingly hot and totally successful arrangement of yellows, bronzes, oranges and reds at its centre. The colour starts in whites at one end and finishes in a bluish haze more than four hundred feet later, *à la* classic Gertrude Jekyll. 'I cut my teeth on that border,' said Rachel Lamb, renowned for her planting, particularly at Ballymaloe. 'And I think I've cracked the border thing, though I found the pinks particularly difficult.'

She has indeed 'cracked the border thing' – it's magnificent. It was wonderful too to see so many of the old border stalwarts from the former Shackleton garden at Beech Park in Clonsilla. Unlike most borders nowadays, which are planted in four layers to give all-year interest, i.e. bulbs, perennials/bedding, shrubs and a tree or two, this is designed to bloom only from late spring to autumn. So it can afford to relax and hang out over the long winter, wearing only its protective coat of decaying foliage.

Shanagarry

Until the early part of this century, Ireland was a buzzword in international gardening circles, a horticultural hot spot housing some of the leading botanists of the day. We were celebrated for our botanical gardens, writers, artists and collectors. Our private and public gardens sheltered collections of rare and sometimes unique varieties. Our beneficent climate, mild enough to experiment with growing new and exotic species outdoors, was universally envied.

With Independence we were left with some good architecture and extravagantly beautiful old gardens on grand estates whose owners were burnt out in the Troubles, fled the country or stayed, many of them too broke to hire the armies of gardeners necessary to maintain them. Either way, many wonderful Irish gardens fell into disuse and eventual dereliction as we buckled down to recreating a national identity.

The next fifty years or so were quiet ones for Irish gardening, save for some exceptional plantspeople in private and public employment, who saved many rare varieties from extinction and kept the flag flying quietly at the cutting edge of horticulture. Some of the best gardens in those years of low employment and even lower wages were to be seen on urban allotments and in suburban back gardens, where many old-fashioned varieties of fruit, vegetables and flowers bred by the great Irish nurseries of the past were kept safe.

Any grander gardens being made at the time were either public, as in Lutyens' war memorial park at Islandbridge, or strictly private and not open to the paying public, though many of them are now. By the early '70s the pall of poverty lying over the country lifted as we supped heartily from the EU honey pot. With prosperity came the inevitable renaissance, in gardening as in the other arts.

Now, at the end of the twentieth century, there are increasing numbers of people with money to spend on great gardening gestures. There is a sense of *déjà vu*, an echo of the eighteenth and nineteenth centuries as people all over the country are busy making the grand gardens of the future. Look at Jim Reynolds, a son of the Meath soil, who is working on an epic scale to finish a pair of cascading canals, limewalks and belvederes in a field in Trim.

Armed with £4 million in EU funds, the Great Gardens of Ireland Restoration Scheme is another side of the same coin. Long-lost gardens and lands have been found again, and their owners encouraged to bring them back to life for opening to the public.

And down in the village of Shanagarry, Co. Cork, where Darina Allen has her cookery empire and the potter Stephen Pearce his lofty, airy Emporium, making gardens on a grand scale seems to come naturally. Which is probably not so surprising when you know that Shanagarry translates as *Sean Gairdín* or Old Garden and has a mediaeval castle with walled garden to boot.

On their sixty acres running down towards Ballycotton Bay, Stephen Pearce and his wife, Kim-Mai Mooney, are restoring and rebuilding their William Penn castle, the sixth redevelopment in its six-hundred-year history. Stephen and Kim-Mai's friend Roger Phillips, the noted plantsman and author, is designing a formal garden in period. An orangery and apple walk are planned and up at Stephen and Kim-Mai's house, baby orange trees are being nursed along in the sunny greenhouse, where plum and cherry tomatoes have been re-seeding themselves for years.

Mediaeval castles and gardens are cutting-edge stuff. But what is truly amazing is Kim-Mai's own pet project, an enthralling young maze of five thousand beech trees, based on a Celtic design taken from the sixth-century Garryduff Gold Bird pin, a sweet little gold wren just fifteen millimetres across. Ten years ago, when she moved to Shanagarry, Kim-Mai became absorbed by gardening, and then mazes, which she had loved as a child. Resolving to make one, for the landscape and for the amusement of the many families who visit the pottery every year, she cast around for a motif that would reflect the maze's natural surroundings, particularly the important bird sanctuary on the edge of her chosen one-acre site, a field where carrots had been grown successfully for years. Stephen's godfather, the artist Patrick Scott, pointed her towards the local bird, housed in the museum in Cork.

She wanted the paths wide enough to accommodate a parent with pram. 'We laid them out according to the bird's own beautiful swirling and circling designs, using its prominent eye as the goal of the maze,' she says. 'But when we were trying to fit it all in to the contours of the land, the bird began to elongate and from certain angles looked strangely like a fish. So now it also celebrates Ballycotton Harbour and its fishing industry.'

'I'm not sure if it's a bish or a fird,' grinned Stephen, 'but I do know it's the first maze to be planted in Munster.' (A second, younger one in yew has since been planted nearby at Ballymaloe.) 'And it's the first to be planted in Ireland in a hundred years, not counting the Beit one at Russborough, which is a very plain affair, also in beech, in the shape of a diamond.'

Kim-Mai's friendly but challenging maze is only in its third year but bushing up nicely. It is now tall enough at four feet to get temporarily lost in, already a place apart from the world as you hunt your way through its interior in the state of heightened awareness brought on by such places and pursuits.

'I reckon it will take twenty minutes to puzzle out the maze. It will be pollarded at two metres so it doesn't become too dark and daunting,' said Kim-Mai, who knows it better than anybody, having first drawn it to scale, pegged out the full field at eighteen-inch intervals and then tied it all together with blue and yellow nylon rope, running in different directions.

'There is a trick to all mazes, but I've overcome this with another trick,' laughs Kim-Mai. 'I'm not going to make it too easy to get to the goal, though there will be few dead ends so people don't lose impetus. I'll plant clematis and roses along the way, but nothing should be recognizable should they lose their way.'

Airfield

When Miss Naomi Overend died without issue four years ago at the age of ninety-three, her death signalled the end of a long and colourful chapter in the social history of Dublin, and Dundrum in particular. For more than a hundred years the Overend family had lived at Airfield in a quiet, idyllic setting on the outskirts of the village, one foot on the edge of the city beside the old Harcourt Street railway line and the other at the base of the Dublin Mountains.

There they kept a sizeable indoor and outdoor staff and worked a fifty-acre farm, whose picturesque fields and meadows are bounded by ancient hedgerows, shown in an 1837 Ordnance Survey map and unchanged to this day. The Overends were famous for their charitable works, their exhibits at horticultural shows, their erratic parking of the Rolls down in the village streets (one of a vintage car collection now being restored for display), and a prize-winning herd of Jersey cows, each one named after characters in the operettas of Gilbert & Sullivan.

Always of a compassionate and pioneering bent, the Overends ensured that their considerable fortune and assets would continue to be used for the public good after their deaths. Long before then, Naomi and her much older sister Letitia (1880–1977) put the necessary legal structures in place to ensure that their beloved home would be preserved intact. A charitable trust now administers the estate, which will be used in future for educational purposes.

After Naomi's death in 1993, the contents were sold off in a one-day auction, which created a minor sensation when £1.4 million in total was bid. As a consequence, the poor house is almost totally denuded, just a footstool here and a few mismatched chairs there. The rather grand library comes as a bit of a shock, with large dark scars left on the walls where bookcases, custom-made by the famous Dublin cabinetmaker James Hicks, were stripped out and sold.

The rest of the public rooms are big, bright, airy and under careful restoration. The library is to be turned into a tearoom, with french windows leading down wide stone steps into the walled garden. Recently redesigned with aplomb by Arthur Shackleton, it boasts among its remaining original features some delicious old Irish apple varieties trained against the walls.

The Overend women were keen gardeners all and the care and improvement of the gardens after their departure was firmly stipulated in the terms of the trust. With the help of the £1.4 million from the auction, the deeply pleasant gardens at Airfield, with their wonderful views over meadow, mountain and rooftops, are being remodelled, restored and restocked and, along with a new retail nursery selling plants propagated from the garden, will open to the public in spring 1999.

After a rest of two years, the farm will be worked again by the same farmer, Donal Lester, and a herd of Jersey cows will once more take pride of place. In a large area behind the walled garden a big, ornate glasshouse has been restored and is waiting to receive tender plants and ferns, for its original Victorian fernery. A sweet little melon house, built half below ground and guarded by a gigantic agave that spends its winters outdoors, houses one enormous cactus while it waits its turn for a makeover. The rest of this area, conveniently near the farm and manure end of things, is a large arable space waiting to be turned into an organic fruit and vegetable garden. The produce of this future garden will eventually go on sale at source.

The present head gardener is Jimmy Blake, one of the new breed of plant-loving working gardeners trained at the Botanic Gardens and now employed in looking after and improving old gardens all over Ireland. Four years ago, when Naomi was still living in the house with a battery of retainers, he arrived to work for a season under the old head gardener, in accordance with the Overends' tradition of employing one permanent gardener as a member of the household and one seasonal one for the busiest months.

Jimmy took over when the older man retired, and though he is just twenty-five years old he is already steeped in the lore and gardening traditions at Airfield. Like those before him, he lives in the pretty gate-lodge, where he has made a cheeky front garden dominated by the half-hardy, orange to scarlet annual *Leonotis leonora*, the unusual 'Staircase' variety. This upright but rather spiky beauty, which flowers usefully from autumn until winter, has soared to seven or eight feet from a packet of Thompson & Morgan seed. Collecting seed from it can be a prickly business.

Still in keeping with the Overend tradition, dating from a more leisurely era, Jimmy had his own, highly praised seasonal gardener for three months this summer. But now he is back working alone and the pressure is on to get the gardens looking wonderful for their first public appearance. Between trimming the yews, planning shrub and dry-shade borders, and planting up the balmy south border which is edged in box and divided by a fledgling hornbeam hedge, he certainly has his work cut out for him.

Jimmy's great allies have been a whole shedful of beautifully rotted Jersey cow manure, professional gardening colleagues willing to swap cuttings and seedlings of good named varieties, and a wonderful big polytunnel for propagation. In this womblike place he also nurtures his own fascinating collection of plants, grown from seed he collected on a trip to Australia, plants which will eventually grace the glasshouse.

But Jimmy Blake really has nothing to worry about. His dedication, skill, and palpable love of plants, combined with a naturally good eye and a questing plant-collector's mind will ensure that Airfield will be a place of great interest for even the most sated garden visitor. There will be no big development, no ugly lavatory blocks, no intrusive car park. Airfield has immense charm and is further graced by mature trees, an avenue of clipped yews and superb hedges of hollies, one curving. It is old-fashioned rural Dublin at its best. And, according to the terms of the Overend trust, it will remain that way.

Already the nearby schools use it for nature and photography trips. But right now the skilfully laid old hedgerows are laden with almost seedless blackberries, the sweetest you'll ever taste and, still keeping within the Overend tradition, it's that time of year when the gates are opened and the local children are invited in to pick them.

National Botanic Gardens

Gardeners work in four dimensions, the fourth dimension being, of course, time. That's why it's vital to know what is good when. Luckily enough, the Botanic Gardens at Glasnevin is a fully stocked four-dimensional reference library where you can go and see not only which plant when, but also where, how and, if you're lucky enough to get chatting to the gardeners, why.

At any time of the year it's wonderfully informative, a place to watch the seasonal changes in a vast range of rare and common plants, from the lowliest grasses to the grandest oaks, and to see in action what you should be doing now, and admiring now, in your own garden. Almost all the plants are labelled clearly, and some carry a short history along with the common and Latin names.

It was all hard work up at the Botanicals last week, where small armies of gardeners, melting under the hot sun, battled against time to finish bedding out hundreds of Dahlias and chrysanthemums for a later show, against the background noise of building and restoration works, which will include a public car park on the spot where the old potting sheds, cold frames and junior orchid house are now, sheltered from the public gaze by high walls and hedges.

New little architectural features have been appearing, some of them blending well with and even enhancing their older surroundings; others, like the raised circular seat facing the gable door of Turner's beautiful curvilinear glasshouse, are a great idea in themselves, but make heavy use of inappropriate building materials. A stiff, dead and deeply dull modern red brick has no place in the company of all that graceful, creamy white metal, curved glass and soft stone.

In the summer, when there is so much to see, a two-hour voyage round the Botanic Gardens is a real adventure, but it's not nearly long enough to take in everything. You need to return again and again, or make a day of it and bring your lunch. Lunching in the Botanics is popular with local shop, factory and office workers, who all seem to obey a marvellously creaky and metallic old bell which calls the gardeners back to work at two o'clock.

Make a note in your diary to visit in mid-June next year, even if it's only to see the long, deep border of massed irises standing completely alone, *à la* Monet. I counted dozens of varieties, all of them in full bloom against the backdrop of a high, imposing hedge of trimmed holly. In June too, you can watch the double herbaceous borders unfold along their immense, box-edged lengths. Though plumping out with promise, the borders are not yet at their peak, but were enlivened by giant, slightly mad and frazzled red poppies, tall spires of blue delphiniums, the sweetly scented Victorian tranquilizer, *Valerian phu*, and the rapidly rising giant grey *Onopordum nervosum*.

The grandly-titled Laburnum Walk doesn't, alas, have a huge number of laburnums, but they are massively underplanted with a clashing though intoxicating range of columbines (*Aquilegia*), best seen in very early summer. Last week the lilacs had just gone over and *Philadelphus, Deutzia, Paulownia tomentosa* and the pendulous flowering branches of *Cercis siliquastrum* were moving centre stage.

While one of the rarer Belizean specimens was waking up to fleeting flower in the balmy orchid house, down in the long grass of the magnolia garden, which is separated by a clematis walk from the symphony in massed irises, nature showed her claws; there, the peace was shattered by a viciously physical fight between a plucky mother thrush and a marauding magpie intent on emptying her nest of young. Happily the thrush won the battle, thoroughly routing the would-be thief without dropping the juicy worm she carried throughout.

One of the things you should see is the formal herb garden, with its pretty urns and box-edged beds cut on an angle, which is now lovingly tended after years of near dereliction. Or if you're plotting revenge and need inspiration, you can always head straight for the poison garden, where noxious plants are labelled 'poison to man', or 'poison to man and animals'. Or choose a lawn from the slabs of different grasses laid down near the vegetable garden; Timotei perhaps, which is used in Scandinavia to thread wild strawberries into necklaces and thus prevent them from being crushed while collecting.

The bog and Burren gardens are interesting, the former with its proper old bog road made of floatable split wood, the latter dominated by raised alpine beds and old white species roses. It's too late for the wisteria, but you can go down towards the river and marvel at its twisted trunks, as thick as your thigh, winding around their iron supports. The gardens are ten minutes from the centre of town, and open every day of the year, except Christmas day. Admission is free and buses, which stop across from the entrance, have proved pretty reliable.

Deutzia

National War Memorial Garden

South of the Phoenix Park at Islandbridge, tucked between the Liffey and the new motorway, lies the Park's beautiful little sister, Sir Edwin Landseer Lutyens' Memorial Garden. Once part of the great park itself, its twenty acres were set aside by the Free State government for a memorial to honour the generation of Irish, 49,400 in all, who lost their lives in the 1914–1918 Great War. When the Board of Works began excavating in the 1930s, they found a Viking burial ground, complete with skeletons and artefacts. The garden was officially opened on Armistice Day 1940, though the public was only allowed in once a year, on Remembrance Day.

By the time the great Lutyens (1869–1944) was commissioned by the Free State to design the garden, he had left behind the Arts and Crafts movement, the William Morris-inspired cosy Utopian vision he had drawn on in many of his complex, pre-war country-house collaborations with the gardener Gertrude Jekyll. He had triumphed with his designs for New Delhi, commissioned by King George V, and was working at his peak in the humanist or classical tradition for his celebrated war memorials.

Lutyens had reached a level of abstract precision and balance, with all the gravity and clarity of ancient Rome, in spirit if not in form. The Dublin garden is a high point in his art and deserves to be better known. Perhaps the reason for its obscurity lies in the fact that it was not open to the public until 1988, Dublin's millennium year, after it had been restored by the OPW. Before that, when anti-British sentiment was running high in the '70s and '80s, it was vandalized by IRA sympathizers. They tried, but failed, to blow up the Gothic cross. Original teak Lutyens benches, with carved regimental insignia, were smashed and shoved into the river. Ditto some of the neo-Palladian columns that form an integral part of the memorial design.

Now the garden is open from dawn until dusk, seven days a week. (In fact, the wicket-gate entrance is open twenty-four hours a day.) It is a place apart, a place of calm for the heart if mourning or troubled. Or for just walking the dog by the river while watching the Trinity College rowers or entire extended families of ducks and swans. The river is on your right as you go in, and the sound of water gushing over a weir drew me in that direction first, away from tantalizing glimpses of architecture and the noise of the motorway on the other side.

The river path goes on for miles, stretching along the wilds of the Liffey Valley Park. But for our purposes we turn left at the railings that bound the garden, and walk along a straight path lined with deciduous trees backed with sombre stands of evergreens. Ahead is the pagoda bandstand, as it is known, a pillared and domed affair completed only last year to Lutyens' design. The OPW's database has his original drawings, dated 1934, and these also include a design for a bridge over the river, which would be a wonderful addition. Five tree-lined avenues radiate from the dome, which is ringed with reproduction Lutyens benches made of sturdy metal. These are cold to sit on but good to look at, and if some more of these were used in place of the picnic benches by the river path it would be a further improvement.

One of these paths, planted with young limes, leads directly up and away from the river. Head up two flights of wide granite steps with limestone-capped terraces, past huge bays, gloomy *Garrya ellipticas* and splayed *Cotoneaster* and you've arrived at the *pièce de résistance*. Here two vast, brimming fountain bowls, with central obelisks representing huge candles, stand on either side of the War Stone, which is used as an altar for non-denominational services. Behind this looms the great Gothic cross, with more steps leading up to a great view over the valley, one of many wonderful views on offer, particularly with the acres of trees all around.

On either side of the 'candles', echoing each other in perfect symmetry, are two pergolas, with lavender under foot and newly planted wisteria and clematis climbing the columns. Four pavilions, representing the four provinces of Ireland, support each end of the pergolas, whose wooden roofs, when covered in the climbers, will represent once again mattresses for the dead soldiers. Records are kept in the pavilions, or Book Rooms.

The twin pergolas and pavilions open out on either side to perfect, circular and tiered rose gardens, with a sunken lily pond at their centre. Over four thousand roses, of similar varieties to those originally specified, have been planted. New herbaceous beds ringing the roses are being prepared by the head gardener and look promising. There are seats placed in the most attractive spots, but on the day I visited the garden was almost empty except for a handful of children playing. Yesterday was Poppy or Remembrance Day, the crowds came, wreaths were laid and the dead of both world wars were honoured.

THE GARDENER'S CALENDAR

January

The Christmas–New Year marathon is over and not a minute too soon. Frayed nerves, family skeletons released from cupboards, those unbearable tensions usually simmering on the back burner brought abruptly to the boil: nothing sharpens your appetite for the garden like a bit of seasonal proximity to family and friends.

The answer to 'What can I do in the garden now?' is: lots of things. Listen to the sweet, calming chatter of the songbirds for a start. Admire the strong green shoots of early bulbs pushing through the soil, the extraordinary light and shadow at play this cold month. If your intention is just to fiddle about with weeds and cutting things back, then you'll stay cold unless you make a bonfire and keep it fed. Very pleasant that, on a still winter's day – and you can use the resultant potash straight away in the garden, particularly around fruit trees. Potash balances nitrogen and hardens plants against frost and fungal diseases.

Set yourself a seriously physical task, such as carting or rolling big stones, shifting piles of earth from A to B for making new beds, or digging foundations for walls, paved areas and other hard landscaping jobs. You'll soon be as warm as toast and stripped down to your shirt sleeves. When you get too hot, try some gentle pruning of fruit trees. Remove any weak, straggly or interlocking branches, aiming for an open, cup-shaped centre, and cut back side shoots (laterals) on summer-pruned trees to about two or three dormant buds.

It's a bare time in the garden, the perfect time for drawing in missing verticals to add structure and shape, for making new plans and reassessing and remodelling old ones. If you're lucky enough to have a decent shed you could just sit there and sharpen the shears while you calm yourself with seed catalogues and fantastic colour schemes for summer. If the weather allows, that is if the ground is not frozen or soggy, you can make forays from your shed to move something herbaceous to a better place. Or plant the tulip and lily bulbs you've just found abandoned under the work bench.

Luckier still is the gardener with both shed and lightly heated greenhouse to play in for the winter. Heating a greenhouse to a degree comfortable enough to work in needn't be expensive with one of those ever-improving oil heaters made specially for the purpose. In the exalted company of winter beauties such as the white, sweetly scented *Jasminium polyanthum*, you can get on with the business of cleaning pots and seed trays, planting up containers for standing near the house, mixing up potting mixtures, sowing sweet peas if you didn't do it in autumn, checking cuttings and attending to the dead-heading and watering of plants in flower.

Except for the very coldest parts of the country, it is okay to plant shallots now. Set the bulbs six to nine inches apart in shallow drills in well drained soil and cover all but the tips. Don't press them down into the soil or you could damage the bulbs. Rhubarb too can be planted, placing stools about three feet apart with their tops about one inch below the soil, which should be well manured or composted. Don't pick it in its first year. Established rhubarb can be covered for early forcing.

Late-flowering clematis can be cut back to three feet from the ground. This will promote flowering at eye level and lower, and demolish that tatty bird's-nest effect to boot. It's important to patrol the garden, checking to see if any newly planted things have been lifted by the frost and stamping them back down if they have. It's wise too, when there's not much growth to get in your way, to check all stakes, ties and wall wires and fix them if they've come loose.

If you are new to gardening and your window looks out on a blank canvas, you are lucky, really. You have the chance to decide exactly what you want from your garden before you've planted or built anything. Much better than planting willy-nilly with any old thing and then having to dig it all up again. The first thing to decide is what you want the garden for, who it has to accommodate, how much privacy you want and what atmosphere you want to create.

Before making your mark on it, sketch out your questions in words and pictures on a piece of paper and the answers will gradually reveal themselves.

∾

Keep digging whenever you get the chance, incorporating as much organic matter as you can lay hands on. There's still time for the frosts to break down compacted clods. Most desirable plants must have a rich, loose soil in which to spread their roots or they will curl up and die.

∾

Now is a good time to take cuttings of yew, if you're lucky enough to know someone who'll give them to you. If not, then buy a bushy mother plant, or two, and use them for making new stock. Yew makes the best hedging of all, but is expensive to buy in any quantity. It is slower-growing than box, but well worth the extra wait.

∾

Plant trees, shrubs and roses if the weather is dry and mild enough. Remember the golden rule: a penny for the plant, a pound for the planting hole, so prepare the site very well and be generous with the bulky organic stuff.

∾

Keep weeding. To paraphrase the Jesuits, it will save you endless work later in the season if you catch them while they're young.

∾

Seed and bulb catalogues make heady reading in the dark of winter. Order seeds now to give yourself a treat through the post.

∾

Continue to keep house-plants warm and draught-free but away from direct heat, though the rather blowsy indoor florists' cyclamen like it cool. Water azaleas from the base with rainwater and never let them dry out completely, unless you want them to die.

∽

Plant deciduous hedges during mild, dry weather. If it turns frosty before you get them in the ground, keep them in a frost-free place in the interim and cover their roots with straw or some other insulation.

∽

If ponds with fish in them are frozen over, the fish will run out of oxygen and die. Ensure there is always an ice-free area, using boiling water when necessary. Alternatively, some people people recommend floating a ball on the surface to keep the ice open.

∽

If you haven't already done so, send mowers and other tools you can't manage yourself to a professional for an overhaul. If you had a goose over the holidays and haven't used up all the lovely white fat on fried potatoes and bread, then try using it to oil your tools. It's very effective as a shield against rust.

∽

If you are planning a seed-sowing campaign, then it's time to scrub pots and trays, inside and out, in readiness. I use an old washing-up brush and a weak solution of Jeyes Fluid and sudsy washing-up liquid. Rubber gloves are necessary when using Jeyes. Encrusted pots and trays harbour all sorts of disease and other horrors, not least the totally disgusting larvae of the vine weevil.

∽

Writing about the weather in relation to gardening practice is a risky business. When I sat down to write, it was a classic January. Gale-force winds were causing ceaseless chaos throughout the country. Houses and gardens were badly hit and more than one professional grower was devastated by the scale of the damage to their glass houses and polytunnels. The only work that could be done outside was clearing up the mess and trying to secure things in danger of being damaged or blown away.

Just as it seemed there was no end in sight, that the only thing left was a fling until spring with melancholia and imagination, everything suddenly changed and a perfect gardening day was born. On that one glorious day smelling of spring, a feisty young breeze dried out the top inch of soil and blew away any lingering traces of Christmas cabin fever. With temperatures reaching 15 degrees centigrade and the soil workable, a sort of delirium set in for the day. Anything was possible, but where to begin?

After walking around picking up kindling for the fire and inspecting for storm loss (limited to one mature rosemary bush), the next thing I did was stab a huge old cyclamen corm, *C. hederifolium 'Alba'*, right through the heart with a hand fork. A miserable experience, and all my own fault for not labelling it properly. How quickly we forget our gardens if we don't have regular contact. Those cyclamen, a gift from a French garden, were only planted out in December.

Weeding was much more fun, while finding and destroying the young slugs feeding off tulip tips, irises and day lilies was a strong palliative for the pain and guilt of the cyclamen incident. Second-year foxgloves were moved to their flowering positions in the belief they'll be white and the silver-leaved New Zealand daisies, *Celmisia*, were given a new collar of grit to ensure the sharp drainage they need to survive.

The unfairly named Stinking Hellebore, *Helleborus foetidus*, a handsome, strong plant with palest green flowers and very dark, finely-cut palmate leaves, had never looked better. This hellebore is so good and so completely able to withstand all weathers and some of the worst positions in this garden that I'm thinking of using it as a sort of low, evergreen hedging or edging to give structure in winter to difficult places. The idea that winter has to be a mournful time for gardens is silly. Some people find bare earth restful, others need to see things going on all the time. Either way, you choose what's happening in your garden in winter by planting what you want to see.

The landscape all around needn't be flat and empty, even for those of the bare-earth school. There are plenty of obliging plants that can change the picture and make winter as interesting a season as any other. If your garden is a mess now, don't be defeated, just resolve to try harder for next year. Make a note of the name of any plant you see now and would like to use. It's a good time to buy hellebores, when they're in flower and you can see what you're getting.

❧

Spring is only a few weeks away. The rays of the sun are growing stronger, there's a big stretch in the days and darkness does not fall until 5 p.m. When it does come marching in, we'll all be back on the gardening merry-go-round, chasing nature but never catching up. All over Ireland, millions of snowdrops, daffodils and aconites are sitting up already, wide awake and smelling the coffee. They can't all be wrong.

There are lots of things to think about now. The birds are hungry, poor things. My friend who is a committed bird-feeder tells me that because of the high winds, they cannot reach the tall food tables in her garden. The wind just lifts them up and tosses them around in the air until they are dizzy and tired. She has seen this happen even with the bigger crows. 'If the birds do eventually reach the tables,' she says, 'the food must be something really good, because they will have used up all their energy getting to it.' She recommends temporarily moving your feeding stations to a more sheltered spot, while keeping an eye out for cats.

This winter the garden has been a riot of tits, robins and blackbirds. Blue tits in particular seem partial to the dried flowerheads on the lavender bush, which, being Mediterranean, is left unpruned until spring for its own protection. Birds are prepared to work for you in return for extra rations. On a day when the soil is not too wet, stir it gently to loosen the surface, particularly around emerging plants and in any other place where slugs lurk. Rout them from their hiding places, expose them to the hungry birds. Unfortunately, birds like beneficial earthworms too, but that can't be helped.

January

There's no reason not to have a succession of bulbs flowering in the house all through January and into early February, before the spring show gets going outside. I find it handy to have a supply of pots planted with different bulbs waiting in the wings outside. They can be brought in at any time over the winter for forcing into early flower. It doesn't have to be anything fancy. Just a shallow bowl of snowdrops is a sensational sight and sweetly scented. The flowers last for about two weeks and the whole lot can be stuck outside again when they've finished, or planted in the green into the open ground where they'll start multiplying almost immediately.

February

Fancy eating fresh sweet strawberries from your own garden this summer? Besides being infinitely better than shop-bought fruits, they'll be soothingly organic to boot. Heavy yields and disease resistance are qualities which have been bred into modern varieties at the expense of flavour, but good organic cultivation has been known to improve them.

Planting times for strawberries are March to April and again from July to October. The ground should be prepared about a month in advance, which means now, so do that before you set off enquiring after good, virus-free strawberry plants or runners. If you live in a wet district, choose varieties that hold themselves naturally upright, to keep the flowers and fruit trusses clear of the ground.

Most varieties make neat plants with attractive foliage and look very decorative when hung with ripening fruits. Apart from growing them in rows or grouped in beds, you can grow them in pots, hanging baskets or those beautiful big Ali Baba strawberry jars which have planting holes all around the sides. They can also be used as a sort of carpet bedding, perhaps enclosed by a dwarf evergreen hedge of box, or by edgings made of parsley, chives or a frilly lettuce.

Alpine strawberries have much smaller leaves and fruits, make compact bushes and can also be used as edging or for mixing prettily with smaller flowers. Alpines enjoy light woodland shade and could also be grown under fruit trees. The large-fruited varieties prefer full sun. All strawberries prefer soil rich in organic humus – manure, compost, leafmould, etc. – which does not dry out in summer.

∾

Now is a good time to divide and increase your stock of *Cymbidiums*, or those other terrestrial orchids, *Cattleyea* and *Odontoglossum*, which have become terribly popular since people realized how easy they are to grow without specialist knowledge or hothouse conditions.

Despite their delicate demeanour, these orchids do not like to be mollycoddled. As with dividing the blue African Lily, *Agapanthus*, a firm hand is needed, which suits them very well. When the roots of *Cymbidium* have become very congested, which they eventually do, and the plant has also produced several leafless bulbs, it's time to divide.

Give the pot a good few whacks to loosen things up. If it has got too overcrowded, you might end up having to break the container to free the plant. Shake off any surplus compost to get a good look at the roots. If they are hopelessly entangled and it's not possible to pull the plant apart into sections with your hands, then take a big, serrated bread knife and slice it in half, roots and all, and halve it again if it's a very big plant. Each section to be re-potted should have at least three good leafing bulbs, known as pseudo- or green-bulbs. Cut off any dead roots with a secateurs and trim the others with a sharp knife. Any leafless bulbs, known as back-bulbs, can also be removed and potted on separately into three-inch pots. Discard any shrivelled back-bulbs and use only those that are firm to the touch. Within a few months they'll produce new shoots of their own.

Make up a very gritty new batch of compost. Orchids need particularly good drainage. Specialist mixtures can be bought ready mixed, or you can make your own. The recipe is: three parts (by volume) of peat or a fibrous substitute; three parts coarse grit; and one part each of perlite and charcoal. Use a pot one or two sizes bigger than the old one, to allow for a couple of years' growth.

To further assist drainage, fill the first quarter of the pot with crocks, small sharp stones or even broken bits of polystyrene. At this stage the compost mix should be quite dry. With one hand hold the orchid section, keeping the oldest pseudo-bulbs towards the back of the pot. Orchids grow out from the front, so this way there's room to accommodate any new development.

Plant so that the crown is just below the rim of the pot and pat compost around the roots, tapping the pot sharply a few times to settle it. When you're satisfied the orchid has got a foothold, water it really well and leave it alone for a fortnight in a cool (not cold) shady place until it recovers. Thereafter, watering should be frequent enough to prevent the soil from drying out, but not frequent enough to make it soggy.

∞

One of Alexander Buchan's cold periods is due, around 7–14 February. Just in case the Scottish Victorian meteorologist, famous for predicting hot and cold periods, is right again, we should be preparing for some of the coldest nights of the entire year. It would be wise to take precautions against severe frosts, just in case.

∞

Snowdrops, crocuses, aconites and any other little bulbs that have struggled through the winter can be rewarded now with a sprinkling of bonemeal or another dry, organic fertilizer. Lilies, tulips, celmisias and anything else that likes good drainage should be given a collar of grit or sharp sand to keep its neck dry.

∞

A thick mulch of anything to hand (rotted manure and garden compost are two of the best), while the ground is good and damp, will give a boost to your plants and keep them moist in dry spells.

∞

The sooner in February you plant fruit and other deciduous trees and shrubs, including roses, the better. But this should not be done if the soil is waterlogged, because walking on wet ground does terrible damage to its molecular structure. Roses can be pruned and tied in now, remembering the golden rule: the weaker the shoot, the stronger the pruning.

∞

New lilies can still be planted outside and established ones transplanted from one part of the garden to the other. All lilies require sharp drainage, so lay them down on a bed of sand and work plenty of sand or other gritty matter into the soil around them. If transplanting, the lilies will be in growth and should be treated in the same way as herbaceous perennials: lifted carefully, with a good ball of soil around the roots.

Madonna Lily

∾

February is the beginning of the new year for those who want to grow vegetables. You start with shallots, those delicious little members of the onion family that are a staple of French cooking but rather expensive to buy here. No special preparation is needed if the ground is in fertile and friable condition. If it's wet and sticky you'll have to wait. Push each bulb into loosened soil, six to nine inches apart, and leave the top third exposed. A sunny spot is best. Onion sets get the same treatment, except that you push the bulbs ever so slightly beneath the surface.

∾

Most snowdrops do well in alkaline woodland conditions, along with hellebores and pulmonarias. Experts say that manure is death to them, so if you're mulching, beware. Strangely enough, this is not mentioned in the generally marvellous new RHS A-Z plant encyclopaedia.

Early snowdrops can be divided now. Propagation is easy enough, by division and self-seeding, though one, *G. atkinsii*, is sterile and has to be increased by bulb division alone. The more fragile ones – *G. sandersii, G. elwesii* and *G. gracilis* – need to be split and replanted every second year, while the more vigorous species can wait three or four years.

The ordinary snowdrop, *G. nivalis*, can be left to increase naturally but by dividing the clumps after flowering, and replanting in groups of three or five, you can speed their spread considerably. Snowdrops are ideal for small gardens, naturalized in grass or in beds and borders, where their dying leaves will soon be masked by the emerging foliage of deciduous shrubs and early herbaceous perennials.

∾

Feed herbaceous borders with compost or rotted manure, spreading it between plants. If these need to be split and replanted, do this before you apply the mulch.

∽

If your herb bed is miles down the garden, it really does make sense during winter to have some herbs growing in a sheltered place near the kitchen in big pots or containers. Parsley can still be dug up and potted, as can mint if it hasn't totally died back. And thyme too, if you give it a gritty, free-draining compost.

Water the herbs an hour before moving if the soil is dry, and lift them with as large a ball of soil as you can manage, straight into their new homes. If you do this in one seamless movement, the plants won't have time to notice and they shouldn't sulk. Of course, this job should really be done in autumn. As for potting up herbs and bringing them into the house, I find they often become infested with whitefly and therefore unusable. A short spell outside usually clears them.

∽

Wipe the leaves of dusty house-plants with a moist, tepid cloth to let the light at them. Feed winter-flowering house-plants once a week but water sparingly.

∽

Start to sow annuals. Some, such as begonias, benefit from an early start but others, such as dahlias, can wait until late spring.

∽

Prune throughout February. After the wisteria and late-flowering clematis, there's buddleia and dogwoods to be cut hard back. As soon as the yellow stars of winter jasmine have faded, take out some of the brown wood completely, making the cuts at the base. You will lose some new green shoots but the plant will be renewed. There's no need to prune it all over. *Jasminum nudiflorum* is a wonderful and long-lasting cut flower for the house.

∽

Now is a good time to plant chives, or divide congested clumps. Simply lift the plants and pull them apart into small tufts. Replant in refreshed soil, in any reasonable soil and a fairly open position, about nine inches apart. They make a good edging plant for many months.

∾

Tulipa turkestanica, the little species tulip from Central Asia, has started to flower in my garden. This is only its second year to flower, and already it has thrown a prodigious amount of seed. Some of these have sprouted where they fell, others I took away and sowed in seed trays, out of curiosity. They flower for a couple of months, giving starry white flowers with yellow centres and robust seed pods. Their dying foliage is screened in summer by the leaves of the small blue hosta, 'Halcyon'. Enjoys lightish soil in sun.

March

'Beware the Ides of March,' a soothsayer warned the ill-fated Julius Caesar, some time before he was stabbed to death in the Senate chamber. If Caesar was a good Roman, then he would surely have been a gardener, and probably thought the old guy was talking about weeds, and the way they start looking at you from about mid-March. Our hero failed to weed out the enemy, and before he knew it, he was surrounded on all sides.

That's what happened to me with the dreaded Japanese Knotweed (*polygonum*: poly = many; gonum = knee or knot). Grateful for any bit of greenery in our first year here, we got quite excited by the exotic knotweed that had sprung up everywhere, carrying its tall plumes of creamy flowers and heart-shaped leaves on reddish stems. We, like Caesar, were a little bemused when an experienced French gardener shook her head in warning against it: 'Non,' she waved a warning finger backwards and forwards. 'C'est pas bon. Non!'

She was, of course, absolutely right, and luckily she sounded the alert before it was too late. It started to come up everywhere, creeping under massed concrete, thriving in the worst and the best conditions. Like the Hydra, when you chop off its head, it grows three more. It is a great destroyer and, as a garden escapee, it has colonized whole stretches of river and roadside. It is now illegal to plant or propagate the knotweed, introduced as an exotic prize by proud Victorians. Our five-year battle against the scourge is almost over, but like one of those Japanese soldiers who periodically emerge from the jungle decades after the war ended, it shows itself red from time to time, still fighting the good fight for emperor and country.

For the unwary, another false seducer is valerian, the insipid pink stuff that eventually destroys old stone walls while seeding itself profusely. Unless you are lucky enough to have the deep red or white varieties, you shouldn't get too romantic about it. Keep cutting it back as hard as you can, and eventually it will weaken. If you pull out the roots by force, tempting as this can be, you'll take half the garden wall with you. It does look pretty in the country, though, and you could give it its head in a wild corner of the garden. This plant carries another health warning: it smells vile indoors.

Another dynamic weed is the dandelion (*Taraxacum officinale*). This stalwart perennial likes deep, good soil, and is a good indicator of where to grow legumes, which favour the same. Try growing some sugar-snap peas there, maybe. A cinch to grow up tripods of cane or pea sticks, they crop for months and are a delicious alternative to those flat little mange-touts. Put plenty of nourishment under them, as they're greedy feeders. Sow directly into the ground from late May onwards. Starting them off in pots earlier seems a bit of a waste of time and space to me, as the outdoor-sown ones soon catch up.

But back to dandelions, which are best tackled individually with a purpose-made, Franco-German 'dandelion killer'. This is a marvellous, long-bladed forged-metal trowel, made in one piece (there are weak-handled imposters), that reaches right down to the deep roots. 'And you too, Brute,' is the war cry as you plunge the killer tool in to the hilt. Very satisfying. A few sharp-tasting young dandelion leaves added to salads makes a good spring tonic.

Then there is the stinging nettle, which used as a vegetable increases blood circulation and is good for teenage spots, apparently. Chickens like them and a clump in a wild part of the garden attracts ladybirds, which then go on to eat aphids.

A weed is a plant in the wrong place, and many of them we've introduced ourselves. Take mint, which some people consider a pernicious weed. You hear experts seriously discussing complicated ways to wage chemical war on this hapless herb. I don't see the problem. What's the big deal if you've allowed the mint too much leeway and it's running everywhere? Just pull it up and out, it's quite obliging and comes away easily. Of course it comes up again somewhere, but it's always welcome in my garden, for its fragrance and flavour. Peppermint makes excellent tea which soothes the stomach, and a leaf chewed as you walk around the garden is refreshing to the palate.

∾

Spring is here. You can smell it in sheltered spaces where the air is still and in pockets of well-drained turned earth. Its scents are soft, rich, full of life and promise. This morning the sun was strong enough to warm the back of my neck – a deeply luxurious surprise. The sharp, wet metal smell of late winter has evaporated in all but the most dank and neglected places, where it will sulk for a while longer before it gets the message.

From now on, longer days warmed by the strengthening sun will heat up and help dry out the soil, making it easier and more pleasant to work. Any excess winter blubber you have stored about your person will start to shift too as you get going in earnest with the spade, the fork, the secateurs, the rake and the shears – all tools you will be needing as spring fever gets a grip.

Though March winds can be cold, strong and north-westerly, often reaching gale force on western coasts and bringing hail, sleet or even snow to the north and high ground, that is no reason to postpone the beginning of the gardening season. Days like that are the exception as the month progresses. Air temperatures often rise to a pleasant 11–12 centigrade and out of the wind's way it can be positively warm and balmy.

Easter is the traditional time when gardeners come out to play. It is far too late to be starting, unless you keep only the barest of low-maintenance gardens. By then the weeds, for example, will have had a head start, whereas if you get them small and before they seed, they're easier to pull, they'll stay pulled for the most part, and root disturbance of valued plants will be minimal.

The garden's own timing is impeccable. Just when it needs your attention most, it makes itself pleasant and fascinating. It races ahead, throwing up surprises to keep you interested. While there is so much to do, and so much time still to do it, you should keep up with it or you could become dispirited. Though February's icy winds tore the santolinas to shreds, laid low the shrubby artemisias and uprooted the smaller evergreens, March's abundance of new growth makes up for all that.

Weeding itself can be a pleasure, an eye-opener. It gets you in close enough to inspect the emerging plants, to exclaim at the new seedlings and admire the old reliables. This year I'm delighted with the strength and quantity of seedlings of foxglove (pure white, I trust) and sturdy *Helleborus foetidissima*, which I'm hoping to naturalize under the difficult canopy of the lime trees along with the existing flora.

Having such an abundance of healthy young plants to hand and for free is quite thrilling and extremely useful for filling in gaps or making new drifts in your own or other people's gardens. But weeding is just one part of the great spring clean-up. When you approach spring cleaning indoors you usually begin by removing the old top layers of dirt, dust and excess bits of baggage of one sort or another. The garden is the same, only much more satisfying. The first thing you do is remove its protective layer of winter clothing, be it leaves, the dried stick-like growth of perennials or the unwanted growth of roses and shrubs. If you have a big garden, cutting back and tidying can be exhausting work for a body made soft by the long, lazy winter.

You don't have to do it all in one fell swoop. The hardier things and those that flower early – pulmonaria, daffodils, tulips, trilliums, geraniums, fritillaries, hellebores and primulas – can be tidied first. Cutting back also lets you rout any slugs, snails, vine weevils or other pests that have been hiding out. It allows you to see what has outgrown its space and needs moving or dividing, or mulching and feeding. For example, roses will be calling for their first meal around about now.

Tenderer penstemons and lavenders needn't be cut yet and something like the South African agapanthus, or dahlias left in the ground, could keep their winter blankets (of wood ash, straw, bracken, fleece or leaves) on for a bit longer, in case we get very severe late frosts. On your voyage of discovery around the spring garden, when everything is still small, it is easier to see where, for instance, a good stand of exotic bamboos would add greatly to the scene, all year round.

❧

When hacking things back it's better to know roughly what you're doing and why. If you make a mistake and prune something at the wrong time, it needn't be fatal, though you will probably lose most of this year's flowers. Clematis are a good case in point. All except the earliest ones look twiggy and a tad messy with no foliage on, so it's tempting to tidy them a bit with the secateurs now.

Don't do it, at least not to the earlies, those that flower before June, such as *C. alpina*, *C. macropetala*, *C. cirrhosa*, *C. armandii* and *C. montana*. Most of these need little or no regular pruning in any case, though some, like the vigorous *montana*, require a major overhaul from time to time to keep them in order. If pruning any in this group, do so immediately after flowering, to give them a whole season to make new stems.

You should, however, take the secateurs to the late flowerers, *viticella*, *texensis*, *tangutica* and the large-flowered late varieties, which flower best on new shoots. Untangle the stems and cut them down to above a pair of developing buds. The *C. tangutica* types have masses of thin, twiggy stems which are a drag to separate. It's perfectly okay to bunch these together and cut through the lot, to about twelve inches from the ground. Feed and mulch after pruning, to alleviate the shock.

❧

Divide and replant congested clumps of snowdrops and aconites to increase their vigour and your stock. Plant in natural-seeming drifts. Herbaceous perennials can also be lifted and divided. Vegetables that can be sown outdoors now, if the soil is workable, include broad beans, lettuce, scallions, some peas, parsnips, Brussels sprouts, radishes, calabrese, spinach and onion sets. In mild areas not prone to frosts, you could risk a sowing of French beans. In the greenhouse, you can sow most of the ingredients for a delicious organic ratatouille: aubergines, tomatoes, peppers and courgettes.

New perennials can be planted now and those in bad positions moved. Trees and shrubs can also go in, if the soil conditions are right. According to a new survey by *Which?* magazine, fertilizers added to the planting hole, particularly bonemeal which is traditionally recommended, can actually retard the root growth of trees and shrubs unless you make sure the soil remains moist. Mulching is the best way to ensure that it does so.

Narcissus

April

The extra hour of evening light, unceremoniously snatched away from us every autumn so that Scottish bravehearts won't have to stumble around in the dark, is back on loan. Why the hardy North Sea dwellers can't change their clocks to suit their own lifestyle beats me. It's unnatural, confusing and doubtless bad for the nerves to have a whole hour thrust upon you at one season and whisked away abruptly at another.

That said, it's a wonderful Easter present for gardeners, who from now on can anticipate staying out till all hours as the light advances. For the rest of the household, though, it usually means increasingly late suppers if the gardener is also the cook. Now is a good time for the gardener to take a stand on the 'who's cooking?' question, and train in any likely successor hanging around the house at meal-times.

Longer evenings make a softly-lit stage for the garden. An evening prowl now with notebook to hand can be both a pleasure and a pain. Whichever it is, take some notes. Early mornings and evenings, before work has started or after it's finished, are good times for thinking and noticing things – and your hands will be reasonably clean then. Otherwise, I find, gardening and note-taking don't mix. The wet muck just loves running into the ink and rendering your jottings filthy and illegible.

This is the time of year when bare patches of earth stare you in the eye. Some of them will be earning their keep to an extent, having maybe a choice late perennial still sleeping beneath. But why are there no bulbs there right now, or a carpet of self-seeding Forget-me-nots?

In a winter landscape the dark brown patches of earth look right somehow, so you forget about them again until spring, when they show up as great big holes in the growing garden tapestry. Lots of ground cover is what's needed, ribbons and pockets and pools of it weaving in and out, drawing in the ground pattern and uniting the permanent planting features.

By ground cover I don't mean the tatty, sprawling 'low-maintenance' shrubs you see languishing in front of modern city office blocks. Instead there are self-seeding annuals like the Forget-me-nots, which look wonderful with scarlet or yellow tulips. Another good carpeter is the evergreen *Gentiana acaulis*, which has shiny, deep green leaves and later gives blue flowers. The wild violets have a delicious scent and should not be banished from the garden for this reason alone. The choicer *Viola labradorica*, with attractive purply-green leaves and deep wine-purple flowers, seems to grow anywhere at all, in light or shade. Any bit of root will take and it's a self-seeder.

Amongst the herbaceous perennials that don't die down completely are the Oriental poppies, whose serrated foliage contributes ferny green or greyish swags of fresh-looking ground colour to the spring garden. *Papaver* 'Fireball', whose later flowers are deep orange, spreads itself around at a great rate and likes to be moved in the autumn. I am always grateful at this time of year for the stature and elegant, upright habit of the tall *ochroleuca* irises, which quickly spread to make a good vertical feature when happy.

Lamiums, the dead nettles, are not all thugs, particularly the silvers, which make a stunning mat in shade. *Lamium maculatum* 'Roseum' has a good pink flower and variegated foliage, and is not over-boisterous. Suitable for this carpeting job too are samples of the sedums, spurges, saxifrages, cyclamen, the potentillas, campanulas, primulas, polygonums, prostrate junipers and rosemarys, the silver lamb's ears, creeping thymes, ivies and jennies, and the low-growing hebes.

∞

For filling late-summer and autumn gaps, sow some fast-growing annual cosmos, which is very obliging with pretty, feathery foliage and flowers in shades of white and deep pink that go on until the first frosts. Nasturtiums too are a good annual filler in sun or shade, and all parts of the plant can be eaten.

There is no mystique about growing from seed, and if you have never tried before, take the opportunity now. It's not too late for most things, even if it says so on the packet. I remember reading about an experiment in the north of England which showed that late-sown seed more often than not caught up with the early birds, flowering at the same time though they had been sown a full month later.

ॐ

Feed roses this month. Plant out sweet pea, pricking out the growing tips to make them bushier. If you didn't sow your own, the nurseries are full of them now.

ॐ

Tie in new growth of roses, clematis, the golden hop and *Solanum crispum*, the potato vine. Divide primroses as soon as they're past their best. If you weren't pleased with the positioning of your *Muscari* (grape hyacinths) this year, move them while they've still got some colour left, which makes them easier to place. Their foliage is often floppy and messy, so perhaps put them behind an early perennial – its emerging foliage will hide them as they die back.

ॐ

Once you've been working outside in the garden it's extraordinary how quickly your sense of smell becomes attuned to the wild, sweet and elusive smells of spring. Go back indoors on a fine day and the first thing you notice are the pockets of stale air lingering on after the siege of winter. This is the time for airing every corner of the house, leaving it wide open to fill up with the freshness carried on every breath of spring air.

It was the smell of common *Myosotis* (Forget-me-nots) in a vase of water that started me off in search of fragrances in the spring garden. It had a slightly faded scent of long, unworried summer after-noons, a scent I'd forgotten in the hurly-burly of becoming an adult. Scent is a bonus at any time but particularly poignant in spring, when the garden is young again, vigorous and fresh after its long rest.

What scents will gladden your heart in the early April garden? Everybody knows wallflowers and their warm, comforting wholesome smell of sweet spices. Every garden should have at least one somewhere, preferably lots. People turn up their noses at daffodils, which is not fair on this most obliging of flowers with its wonderful new smell when freshly picked. It's all the fault of those overbred, virtually scentless shop ones with which we are bombarded.

Another plant that gets good press but shouldn't, in my estimation, is the common flowering currant, *Ribes sanguinem*, which can make a dense, pretty enough hedge if kept trimmed. But, while this over-accommodating shrub always surprises with its early pinkness, I'd rather be surprised by it in someone else's garden. To be crude, it smells of cat pee or cat spray to me and if you must have it – it is reliable and early – then I believe this native of the western United States comes in two other varieties, *splendens* and King Edward VII, which are supposed to be superior in colour and just as easygoing.

Not all the scents of April fit in with the notion that spring is all sweetness and light, delicate and somehow modest, as typified by the soft, almost lemony wild primroses, sweet violets or the evergreen shrub *Osmanthus delavayi*, whose fragrant white tubular flowers carry a clear daytime smell well into the next month or so. Before I even get to the heady, evening scent of the daphnes, consider the downright foxy smell of the fritillaries or the serious, downbeat, powdery saffron aroma that emanates from a crocus when picked.

Clematis are not usually associated with scent, but *C. armandii*, which has leathery, lanceolate evergreen leaves and likes sun, is blossoming now and smells of something elusive but very good. 'Snowdrift' is loveliest, with great swags of white flowers. The rampant, shade-tolerant *C. montana* is budding up nicely at the moment as it prepares to love-bomb us with blossom. While it is always said to smell of vanilla, it most definitely smells of almonds around here.

Some of the April-flowering magnolias, for example *M. sieboldii* syn. *parviflora* and *M. soulangeana* 'Alba Superba', have large fragrant flowers that could play a star part anywhere. Some people, however, say they cannot abide the heavy, waxy funereal quality of the magnolia's cup-shaped flowers. If they have that effect on you but you'd still like a grand display to look forward to in late spring, then *M. stellata*, the star magnolia, is a much featherier variety, though I've never sniffed it and can't find a reference to any scent. A deciduous shrub to ten feet tall, it has silky buds opening to star-shaped pure white flowers, sometimes tinged with pink. In fact, there are lots of magnolias which have softer, more open flowers.

The scent of honeysuckles is not associated with this time of the year but there is at least one kind that flowers now. *Lonicera japonica* is a vigorous, woody, very hardy, semi- or evergreen twining climber with very fragrant white flowers, sometimes flushed with purple, which it carries over a long period, from now until late summer. *L. x bella 'Atrorosea'* is an upright, deciduous shrub honeysuckle which has dark pink flowers in spring and grows to eight feet. 'Candida' is the white version.

Daphne has its troubles, being so attractive to aphids, leaf spot, grey mould (*botrytis*) and troublesome viruses. But because daphnes' scents are attractive to humans, it is particularly welcome at this time of the year when really deep fragrances are so rare. Plant an early flowering one, like *D. pontica* or *D. tangutica*, in a spot you pass on your journey home after dark.

૭

Deadhead daffodils that have gone over. It improves the look of things generally and also stops them wasting their energy on producing seed heads. Do not cut down the foliage, now matter how much it annoys you. Let it die back naturally to feed the bulbs and resolve to move them to a less conspicuous place before next year.

૭

Except for the *Williamsii* types, camellias are notoriously reluctant to shed their spent flowers. I'm afraid the other types will need picking over as they wither, though this is only feasible on smaller plants.

૭

Autumn-sown sweet pea plants can go into the ground this month. Give them a good, sunny site dug with masses of rich, moisture-retentive compost. For a later display, there's still time to sow fragrant sweet pea seed directly into the ground. Indeed, a wide range of hardy annual flowers can be sown outside now, including poppies.

All clematis can be planted now and it's a good time to buy when you can actually see if there is strong new growth. Deep planting, a few inches below the normal soil level, will help if the plant ever succumbs to the mysterious clematis wilt, which strikes swiftly and can ruin a huge, healthy plant in a matter of hours. If the plant is deep, there's a better chance of new shoots springing from the base. Give it plenty of compost and keep its feet in shade, which can be provided by a slab, stones or a mulch.

May

A star of the May garden has to be *Dicentra* in all its forms, but particularly the old-fashioned *D. spectabilis*, with its rosy pendent lockets dangling upside-down on arching feathery stems, and the exquisite white form, *alba*, of which 'Pantaloons' is the most vigorous. *Dicentra formosa* 'Stuart Boothman' is smaller, has blue-green foliage and makes a large, attractive mound quite quickly with less perfect, mauvy-pink flowers. Dicentras are members of the poppy family and will grow in moist semi-shade, perhaps with ferns.

No other garden plant seems to have attracted so many pet names as *Dicentra spectabilis*: Bleeding Heart, Lyre Flowers, Dutchman's Breeches, Lady's Locket, Our Lady-in-a-Boat and my own favourite, Lady-in-the-Bath. If you pull a locket into a different shape, the bath is quite clearly a hip-bath and the lady lifts up her white arms as though performing her ablutions. Vita Sackville-West was even more fanciful, seeing a 'little pink and white ballet dancer', and Edward Lear, in his Nonsense Botany, named it 'Manypeeplia Upsidownia'.

∽

If the oxygenating weed you introduced to your pond is threatening to take over, don't panic. Apparently it tends to do that at first, before settling down. Just yank handfuls of it out if it's getting too cocky, and consider replacing it with a less invasive kind, such as *Ceratophyllum demersum*.

∽

Support emerging tall perennials with sticks or frames which will be obscured by the time the plant is in full leaf. You should have finished pruning climbing and bush roses. Lift and divide congested clumps of hostas and day lilies. To deter greenfly, try planting a few cloves of garlic around the base of any roses susceptible to the blighters and fire basins of soapy water at them whenever you remember. Apparently, washing-up liquids contain salts, so use pure soap, such as Lux flakes.

∾

When tulips have shed their last petals, snap off the nascent seed heads to conserve their energy, as with narcissi. This also encourages stems and foliage to die down more quickly.

∾

Start hardening off trays of bedding by day in preparation for planting out, but remember to bring them in at night. The temperatures can still drop drastically overnight at this time of year.

∾

Sow Brussels sprout seed now for late winter and spring crops. They can be sown in pots and the seedlings pricked out individually when they're large enough to handle. Broccoli, late cauliflowers, spinach, swedes, carrots and winter cabbages as well as greenhouse cucumbers, aubergines and peppers can also be sown now.

∾

It's difficult, but resist putting your outdoor tomato plants into their fruiting positions until the end of the month as tomatoes are extremely sensitive to changes in temperature. While you are waiting for them to harden off thoroughly, prepare their planting site, preferably on the sunny side of a fence or wall where they'll be protected from the wind, while getting any reflected heat from the sun.

Dig in plenty of rich compost or completely rotted manure (this is best done well in advance) and mix in a good dressing of bonfire ash, or potash as instructed on the packet. When they're ready to go in, make a hole with a trowel and set the plants eighteen inches apart if growing in rows, checking that the top roots are no more than half an inch below the soil.

Keep the rootball of each plant intact and firm with your fingers.

At planting time, drive in a sturdy cane and loosely tie each plant to it for support. Water well and mulch with anything to hand, though garden compost or rotted manure is best. All side-shoots, that is those growing between the leaf axils, should be pinched out regularly, though this is not at all necessary on the bush varieties of cherry tomatoes. When the first truss of flowers has set fruit, feeding with a special organic tomato fertilizer pays good dividends.

∾

By late April, barring absolutely freakish weather, any danger of late frost snipping tender plants in the bud is past. So if you're planning to fill pots and containers for a summer show, it's time to get cracking. Plants in pots are portable and therefore very useful for an instant effect. They offer the chance to simulate all kinds of growing conditions, which means you can have combinations of plants that would never be possible in the open ground.

Even a good garden can have its dull moments and pots can provide a great splash of colour, draw the eye away from something lesser and also make it seem that there is more going on than is really the case. That Grand Dame of twentieth-century gardening, Gertrude Jekyll, cheated a bit by getting her private army of gardeners to plunge great pots of flowering lilies into the soil, to fill any gaps in the midsummer borders, making sure any sign of the pots was disguised by the surrounding foliage. It's an excellent idea, actually, as lily bulbs are weak things in many gardens and easily succumb to the depredations of slugs.

Containers also allow you to make a garden where none exists, where there is no soil at all – on balconies, roof-gardens and even inside in a room if placed near the light from the windows. Where there is no garden as backdrop, a solitary container can look very lonely indeed and you'll soon find yourself potting up others to keep it company. However, a really beautiful or strongly shaped pot, say a very large Cretan urn, looks better left unplanted and standing alone.

When a large container is filled with crocks for drainage, then soil and then the plants, it weighs a ton, so it is better to do the job on the site where it will sit for the rest of the year. People with green-houses can start planting theirs a month earlier to get a head start on the rest of us, but they'll need a crane to lift out the big ones. They will also have to be careful when hardening off, as their plants will be soft, fleshy and easily chilled after their plush life indoors. But tender plants are not the only subjects suitable for containers: almost anything can be grown in a pot provided you give it what it needs in the way of soil, food and drink, and herbaceous perennials are particularly obliging, though not often seen.

I'm a bit sick of seeing the New Zealand flax used as the centre-piece of every other containerized scheme. The sword-shaped leaves of the redder crocosmias, like 'Lucifer', or the handsome (for most of the year) leaves of the tall white *Iris ochroleuca*, make a good substitute. Simple dwarf nasturtiums and wild-looking tiger lilies go well with the crocosmias. The more graceful grasses, with their arching ways, also make good centrepieces in a big pot.

It is important to think carefully about colour and what goes with what. If using long-flowering bedding plants like petunias, busy-lizzies or one of the many daisies, don't just mix the colours willy-nilly. If unsure about combinations, remember that you're usually safe with white and that lots of good foliage without flowers will stop things from getting too hectic.

Slow-release fertilizers such as Osmocote are at last generally on sale and no longer the preserve of the professional growers. When mixed in with the potting mixtures, they feed the plants over a period of six months. They are not organic. Unless you're going to be around all the time, or have someone to water when you're away, I would recommend also using some loam, or good topsoil, in the potting mix. This doesn't dry out so quickly, gel or no gel, and pots, particularly those on balconies or roof gardens, are less likely to blow over in a strong wind. To stop moisture and goodness leaching from the pots every time you water or it rains, use some kind of saucer under the pots so they can drink from the bottom up.

June

In their pursuit of truth and beauty gardeners are never satisfied. The garden is never good enough for visitors, who are invariably told how good it was last week, or will be next week. One exception to this behaviour occurs in the month of June, when even the lowliest gardener can boast of at least a bit of colour, even if it's only the yellow-flowering heads of brassicas gone to seed or a few pot marigolds involved in a screaming session with a clump of seriously pink Ragged Robin.

June colour is easy enough for anyone with a modest knowledge of plants: roses, peonies, honeysuckles, Oriental poppies, hardy geraniums, alliums, irises, delphiniums and geums are but a random sample of the flowering plants that epitomize this month. Everything grows so fast in the light and warmth of June that it can be difficult to keep up with it all.

That is all very well for the well-stocked veteran gardener, who can afford to be a bit smug in June when you can't stop things growing and blooming, which they do the moment you turn your back. But for the keen novice with only a smidgen of knowledge and a small stock of plants, it can be a terrible disappointment, full of empty patches or mismatched groupings and with no shape to it at all.

If you can't get it right in June, the doom merchants pronounce, you will never get it right and should stop wasting your time forthwith. That is a depressing thought and one which every gardener has entertained after a particular failure. Don't mind them, but do get out your notebook and jot down what you do and don't like about the garden, and why that is so.

Note the plants you want to increase and find out how to propagate them. Be honest with yourself and don't feel obliged to give a plant room in your garden just because it's alive and growing. If you don't really like it, there's no point. Chuck it out or give it to some-one who does like it. Where height will be needed for the rest of the summer try making tall tripods of canes and plant scarlet-flowered runner beans, sweet pea and nasturtiums to scramble up them in a hurry.

Other gaps can be filled with the taller hardy annuals like cosmos and nicotiana, for colour and scent into the autumn. If you can't relax in your garden in June without noticing all the things that need to be done, then do them now and you can relax and enjoy your bit of creation in the warmer months ahead. Now is a good time to take softwood cuttings from new shoots, preferably in the mornings when the plants haven't fully woken up. Your stock of fuchsias, philadel-phus, hebes, vines, pelargoniums, chrysanthemums, hydrangeas, ceanothus, lupins, chaenomeles, choisya and jasmine can all be increased by this method.

Cut more growing tips than you will need, about six inches long, and put them straight into a plastic bag to prevent water loss. Prepare a really loose compost, with at least 50 per cent sand or vermiculite, or buy a bag of seed and cuttings compost. Trim each cutting to just below a leaf node, strip off the bottom leaves and put six or so around the edges of a pot. Cover with a plastic bag and leave in a bright place until new leaves appear, then pot up individually in a nourishing compost to grow on. Cuttings of perennial wallflowers are easy now: choose lateral shoots and push them around the edges of a pot with the usual 50/50 peat and sand mixture.

Scented garden pinks can be propagated now by means of cut-tings known as 'pipings' – healthy, non-flowering shoots four or five inches long pulled off at a joint. Insert the pipings firmly, two inches deep and four inches apart each way in a sandy soil in a frame, pots or a shady border and keep well watered. They should be rooted and ready for planting out by the end of September. *Chaenomeles japon-ica* (flowering quince) and clematis can be propagated by layering in pots of peat, severing the new plants from the parent a year from now.

Cut back stems of bearded iris after flowering and feed if on poor soil. Prepare a sunny, well-drained spot for any you plan to divide and replant in July or August. Cut out shoots that have just flowered from deutzia and cut broom shoots if you don't want them to seed. Remove the unsightly brown heads of spent lilac and thin out weak shoots. If you like senecio but not its crass yellow flowers, then nip them in the bud.

Keep mulching if you can, to conserve moisture, or else start planning a garden that will survive in drought conditions, which could be fun in itself but rather limiting in the long run. That's enough work. Summer, supple, simple and spacious, is here. Have a break, eat fresh strawberries and listen out for the bumble-bee humming as he gets gloriously drunk on the nectars you've provided.

∾

There is still time to sow peas and French beans straight into the open ground. Water them well. French beans are tender, slender, stringless and best eaten young. Clumps of primroses can still be divided where they are too congested. Except for the bush varieties, outdoor tomatoes, which don't need feeding until after the first fruits have set, should be staked with four- or five-foot canes. Continue sowing salad crops such as scallions, lettuce and radish.

∾

Oriental poppies won't mind being cut right down to the ground after flowering. The perennial cornflower, *Centaurea montana*, is another great sprawler. When it is looking tatty it can be cut back leaving its neat new foliage at the centre. A second, lesser flush of flowers will follow.

∾

Here's a tip from an experienced friend for getting rid of woolly aphis, those awful, sticky puffs of white candyfloss stuff which blight fruit trees. Woolly aphis sets up house anywhere there is a wound. My friend uses pure methylated spirits, carefully dabbed on each one with a long-handled artist's paintbrush, and says it always works.

∾

Raspberries, black currants and strawberries are ready for picking. To guarantee wallflowers or sweet williams in your own choice of colours next year, you could sow seed outside now. After heavy rain is a good time to catch up on your mulching and conserve the moisture in case there's another dry spell around the corner. It is also a good time to divide primulas and polyanthus and replant them in refreshed ground.

∾

Between June and October regulate the blades of the mower according to the weather. When it's very dry, raise the blades and let the clippings lie where they fall to help retain moisture. Remove when they turn brown and unsightly. To finish on lawns: drought can damage yours, but if you spike it well in June and July, ensuring the ground is soft after rain or hosing, it will enable any further water to penetrate deep down to the roots.

July

Somebody once said that 'gardening demands of us that we cannot stand still', and it's true. We must always be doing after it. There are people who wouldn't dream of leaving their gardens in summer when there's so much looking after to do; others down their tools at the beginning of the holiday season in July and don't lift them again until September.

If the garden was splendid in April, May and June, it's easier to rest on your laurels, particularly if you've been provident and clever and filled it with good things for later – penstemons, kaffir lilies, repeat roses, kniphofias, Japanese anemones, shrubby salvias, autumn crocus, red lobelias, crocosmias, asters, sedums, dahlias, rudbeckias, border phloxes, runner beans and lots of good foliage plants.

But those gardeners who stay at home in summer are right (and sensibly take better holidays at a less crowded time of year). If you stand still too long in the face of nature, it will just carry on without you, ruthless in its disregard for any plant that needs cosseting. Amid such chaos the fine thread of a garden, so carefully spun at planting time, unravels and gets lost in the undergrowth. Plants that should be preparing to take centre stage over the next couple of months will instead be dying if not dead, weak and anaemic under foliage that should have been cut back, prey to every snail and slug in the parish. Nature never takes a holiday, nor does it take any prisoners. Left to itself, nature will strangle, starve and take the light from all but the fittest and there'll be little joy in the autumn garden until the ceremonial bonfire. This summer I had to abandon my own patch at a time when the peonies, roses and geraniums were looking after the show. When I returned to it there was a jungle backdrop, a place I hardly recognized.

On either side of the path, threatening to close ranks and swallow it up entirely, were marching columns of tall, pendulous sedge, *Carex pendula*, which has a vicious cutting edge and arrived here of its own accord. Three Alpine strawberry plants had become parents to thirty more and the whole family was camped out, draping themselves over the herb bushes in the sunny, well-drained site where I'd innocently put them for safekeeping.

The hostas were shredded except for their lily flowers, which looked ridiculous standing on their own without foliage. Enormous snails had become so confident that they slept on the remaining stalks in broad daylight. Their energies spent, the Oriental poppies and big geraniums had collapsed into unkempt heaps on top of agapanthus, campanulas and asters.

Climbing roses, *Clematis montana* and honeysuckle were closing in on all sides and a huge stand of the giant busy-lizzy, *Impatiens glandulifera*, a.k.a. Himalayan balsam, was towering over one end of the border, having wiped out an entire wall of raspberries and obliterated the runner beans trained on wigwams.

In short, the garden was a disaster. I had lost touch with it and needed help. I called in the *meitheal*, the traditional working-party used by the Irish under the Brehon laws. My *meitheal* was a party of one, but one who has the eye of an artist and the soul of a serious sweeper. 'OK,' she said before lunch, 'you must move that' – a rugosa rose in the wrong place. 'It's ruining the shape of the bay tree.' She's right, of course. It's a good, clean glossy bay which I've been shaping into a tall spiral, though only on one side because the rose kept growing into the other.

Called 'Hansa', with dark magenta, medium-sized and delightfully scented flowers, the rugosa was given to me as one that grows to three or four feet. Pshaw! It's now seven or eight feet in height and almost as much in width. In autumn, when Hansa has lost the last of her pretty, pale yellow leaves, she'll be pruned down and moved, though I'll take cuttings first as a precaution, in case she doesn't survive transplantation.

It was good to be told what to do for a change. After that decision, I felt better, as though a veil had been lifted from my eyes. 'OK.

We'll start work by sweeping the front paths,' said my one-woman *meitheal*. I doubt a feng shui consultant costing hundreds of pounds could have done any better. Suddenly the front garden had a shape again and it was easy to see what other jobs needed doing immediately. Before she left, she pointed at the pendulous sedge blocking the best brick path at the back of the house. The sedge is a decorative enough form often used in gardens and lovely silhouetted in a lake. 'Get rid of that,' she advised and went home, her only reward a papyrus plant for the edge of her pond.

That evening, in the rain, I started pulling up the sedge in earnest, delighted at how much space I was reclaiming. Little side walls that had been completely hidden by its strapping leaves were once again revealed. After that, everything fell into place and the garden was my oyster again. What amazes me is that it took just three simple ideas to make it so: a major sweep-up, the removal of enough sedge to line a stream, and the decision to move the rose and free the long-suffering bay tree.

∾

Summer pruning of roses consists of picking them for the house and deadheading. Feed them after the first flush of blooms, if you're the nurturing type. Continue cutting back early herbaceous plants and deadheading where there are still flowers. In mild districts, delphiniums and lupins cut to the ground can give a second, lesser display. Don't hack back peonies. Their foliage is ornamental and it should die back naturally as part of the ripening process. Keep picking sweet pea to encourage more flowers.

∾

Don't want to depress you, but autumn is coming, so it is time to think about ordering spring bulbs – the earlier the better.

∾

Prune wisteria to stop its tendrils going where they're not wanted. Choose the growths you want to keep to cover empty spaces and let them coil around the supporting wires. Cut back those growths you don't want to keep, to five or so pairs of leaves. These can be cut again in late winter or early spring.

∽

If you can find them, start planting autumn-flowering bulbs such as sternbergias, colchicums and nerines. Collect ripe seed from any aquilegia you want to increase, then cut back the flowered stems to make room for something else to spread. New, whippy growth on rambling roses and other wall shrubs, such as pyracantha, should be tied into place.

August

I like the garden in August. It has a quieter, less demanding and rather dissolute atmosphere, now that growth has slowed down to a more companionable pace. There are plenty of good, intensely coloured plants coming into their prime this month, strong reds, yellows and purple-blues to add depth. And even if the garden leaves a lot to be desired, it is too late to do much about its apppearance this month, beyond the obvious tasks of deadheading, cutting back, keeping things watered and admiring the apples turning red and gold on the trees.

August for the gardener is a laid-back time, a holiday with some light exercise and lots of time for contemplation, which in turn encourages the flow of new ideas. Take the time to visit other gardens and take note of desirable plants, inspired planting combinations and good design features that could be adapted and carried out in winter.

Looking around my own garden now, I'm pleased with the way last year's massed planting of tall blue, smoky grey and white agapanthus has flowered, their lovely round heads enhancing the whole scene. What I regret most is not buying large quantities of good, Dutch-grown *Allium* bulbs while they were on sale under my nose at the Hampton Court show in early July. The garden could really do with a bit of global glamour from the tall and aptly-named *A.* 'Purple Sensation', or *A.* 'Globemaster', or the pale but impressive *A. christophii*, with its star-studded heads the size of a football. For the moment, I have to make do with *A. caeruleum* and flowering leeks. The latter are nice enough – particularly while the heads are still half-sheathed in tissue-thin minarets – but they are too quiet to make much impact among their purple, red, lime and orange-yellow neighbours.

August is also the perfect time to propagate many plants from cuttings. They are hopping with hormones now and will strike easily. A simple, satisfying job, it demands little energy or financial outlay but pays rich rewards. Hebes, penstemons, rosemary, lavender, box, yew, zonal and ivy-leaved pelargonium, salvia including kitchen sage, artemisia, senecio, hyssop, rue, bay, heathers, hydrangeas, fuchsias, lilac, clematis and semi-tender perennials such as *Felicia* and *Argyranthemum* can be propagated from cuttings now.

Cuttings are taken in three ways. Woody ones are pulled off with a heel attached, softwood shoots are cut cleanly across just below a leaf-node or joint, and some, such as clematis, are cut across half-way between two sets of nodes. Choose pieces that are almost mature and were produced during the current year. Depending on the plant, these can be anything from three to about ten inches long. Remove all the lower leaves to ensure none will be left below ground when they are planted, either in a sandy, free-draining drill in the open ground or in boxes and pots. A John Innes No. 1 compost is ideal, or a 50/50 mixture (by volume) of sand and peat. They don't need nourishment at this stage, just the right conditions to put down roots.

A trick when taking cuttings of zonal and ivy-leaved pelargoniums is to leave them overnight in a dry place in shade to allow them to dry a bit and form a skin over the cut surface. This helps to prevent the stem rotting when it's potted up. Some people prefer to omit this procedure and dip the ends in hormone rooting powder for immediate potting. You could experiment with both methods.

Keep them in a shady spot, out of drying winds, preferably covered by glass or plastic to create a sheltered, water-retentive environment for them, though this is not strictly necessary. Not every cutting roots – if you get 50 per cent you're doing very well – so put in about double the number you think you'll use. By next spring, most cuttings taken now should be rooted and ready for potting-on. Some things may take longer, so if in doubt, just leave them alone for a few more months.

Carnations and pinks can also be increased by layering, though July would have been better. Choose a non-flowering shoot, make a slit in the outer skin on the underside of the stem, pin it down to ruffled soil that's had a little sand added. Water and leave it be for about five or six weeks, then loosen the pin and tug it gently to see if it's rooted. If so, detach the layer from the parent plant, leaving it with half an inch of nourishing umbilical stem, but don't dig it up for transplanting until at least another three weeks have passed.

August is also the time to consider the lilies. The Madonna lily, *L. candidum*, should be found and planted as soon as possible, not more than two inches below the soil, which must be rich and free-draining. Tiger lilies, *L. sargentiae*, produce bulbils after flowering, which are very easy to grow on. You'll find them growing between the stem and leaves. When ripe enough to fall at a touch, plant them two inches apart in a seed box or tray of sandy compost, no more than half an inch deep. Lilies can also be increased from ripe, home-saved seed and will reach flowering size in two or three years' time. Lilies can be temperamental and don't do well for everyone. So if you've got a variety you like, and one that likes you, it makes sense to increase your stock and grow a big stand of them. When the seed capsules have swollen, turned pale and are beginning to split open at the top, they're ripe for sowing.

Cuttings of lavender, rosemary, sage, etc., will root well if taken now. Take three- to four-inch long, non-flowering shoots, remove any bottom leaves and insert the shoots an inch or so apart around the edges of pots filled with sandy, free-draining compost. Water well, and keep them in shade until they root and need potting-on.

∽

If you're a chocoholic on a slimming diet, try sniffing the dark brown flowers of the perennial *Cosmos* 'Atrosanguineus' when the urge to gorge comes upon you. They smell amazingly of good chocolate laced with liqueur, particularly if it's sunny. Just a sniff can ease the craving for the real thing.

∽

After months of flowering, the violas, even the noble perennial *Viola cornuta*, are coming to an end. Shear them now, keeping a patch or two of favourite colours for seeding, and a second, lesser flush of flowers will grace your garden well into autumn.

∾

The stage is now set for the autumn look – a leaner, more stately silhouette, welcome after the chaotic jostling and crowding of the past few months. Now there are fewer flowers to distract and individual beauty can stand out to be admired. Fresh and beguiling new plant combinations are being revealed daily as floppy foliage and spent flower stalks are cut back.

Apples and pears are not the only fruits of autumn, nor dahlias, chrysanthemums and asters the only flowers. Juicy red and purple Victoria plums are easy to grow, and right now my young tree, laden with fruit, looks divine with a stand of tall blue cardoon thistles rising up on the slope behind it.

Gardening in early autumn is a deeply pleasant experience, particularly if there's been late summer rain. Then soil is friable, workable without being wet and sticky. The air is soft, thick and honeyed. It muffles harsh, outside sounds as you work in the shortening days, now lit by a softer light as the sun moves lower in the sky. Growth has slowed down or stopped, but many plants retain their full-grown shape and size, making it easier to plan for the future. Leaf shapes, fruits dangling from their trees and the individual faces of flowers can all be admired to the full now, while there is less competition.

It takes an experienced hand to keep a garden looking gorgeous as it slowly strips back in preparation for a fiery climax at the end of autumn. Every garden should have one tree or large shrub that takes on good autumn colour. A Japanese maple – they come in lots of sizes – would be a good bet for even the smallest gardens. Most of them can get a good blaze going in autumn, but a few stand out from the rest. *Acer palmatum* 'Osakazuki' is one. A strong grower, it has large-lobed leaves that don't scorch in sunshine and change to burning crimson in September and October. Another good acer is 'Seiryu', with red tones when young and gold tints later. 'Senkaki' is also gold but with coral-pink stems that change to red after the leaves have the ground or into containers. Daffodils (narcissi) are one of the most welcome of spring flowers and should go in now, or at least by the end of the month, if they are to get a decent root system established. Dependable and tolerant as the narcissus is, it is still wise to buy your bulbs early, before the best ones are snapped up. Accept only those that are clean and plump and discard any that are dry, shrivelled or mouldy. This goes for all bulbs, except the common bluebell, which seems to grow whatever its condition. If bulbs are at all shrivelled, try rehydrating them overnight in a liquid feed solution. I find seaweed the best feed of all, for everything.

Except for a few forms that will only live on raised beds or against warm, dry walls, there are not many places where the hardy narcissus refuses to grow. This includes in grass, preferably on a rich loam, where they look best planted in large drifts. Though narcissus is not native to Ireland, it seems to have found its spiritual home here, spreading freely wherever it was planted, eventually escaping over the walls of gardens and orchards to become naturalized in the country-side. At the turn of this century, Ireland was renowned for its excellent daffodil collections, particularly those at the TCD and Glasnevin botanic gardens and one containing many precious kinds, kept by a Miss Currie in Lismore, Co. Waterford.

It makes sense to mark the spot where bulbs are planted. Apart from being a terrible waste, it is horrible when the spade slices through a clump of fat, engorged bulbs lying low underground. Even a stick will do, though some kind of a weatherproof label, made of lead or copper, is better. Those with a separate tie-wire are best of all: cut a decent length of coat-hanger wire, remembering that some of it will be lost in the ground. Make a loop at one end with pliers and tie on a name tag.

When planting bulbs in a new, bare place, think even further ahead than the promised glory of their flowers. Think in terms of planting in layers, some herbaceous perennial that will come on after-wards in the same spot and disguise the foliage as it dies back. Bulb foliage – and big daffodils need a good six weeks for this – should always be allowed to die back of its own accord. It makes a rich, nat-

fallen. If your soil is extremely alkaline or exposed, acers probably won't grow on it. Try *Rhus typhina* 'Dissecta', a cut-leaf version of the common stag's horn sumac, which takes on an excellent gold colour. Like all its family it suckers extensively, and where space is limited it is best pruned hard in winter to check its growth.

Bedding out is not confined to summer. Cosmos can be grown in pots and put out when space becomes available in late summer, though I neglected to sow any this year and am now kicking myself. Instead, I'm making do with some glabrous-leaved *Cerinthe purpurea*, the super-fashionable annual, a posh cousin to the yellow-flowered lesser butterwort. Though a perennial, the chocolate-scented cosmos with petals of darkest velvet is great fun to play with and will flower for ages yet. Its flowers look good at the moment with the wide green strap leaves of *Agapanthus africanus*. The tender, ubiquitous bedder *Impatiens* (busy-lizzy) will flower for months in dampish shady areas and looks best if the different colours are kept separate.

They are a bit too busy for me, though I have got an extraordinary little one raised from seed by a friend in England. Aptly named *Impatiens pseudo viola*, its tiny white to pale pink flowers, held erect when open above dainty, serrated mid-green leaves, is indeed viola-like. I'll save the seeds and hope to have a little clump of them for this time next year. Parsley kept in pots as bedding and transplanted out in some formation now, can add good structure near the edge of a path.

If you fancy low-growing mats of dazzling blue trumpets this time next year, search out the autumn-flowering perennial gentian *G. sino-ornata*. It starts to flower towards the end of August and continues on until Hallowe'en. Its brilliant blue is a perfect, finger-high foil for stone. Give it a home in a well-drained, lime-free rock garden or raised bed, where it will increase rapidly if kept from drying out. Like camellias and other plants from acid habitats, it much prefers rain to tap water.

If you're lucky enough to have a wildish, boggy place with rich soil and some shade, a place suitable for candelabra primulas, then *G. ascle-piadea*, the willow gentian, is the one to grow there. About eighteen inches high, it has a slightly wild look and carries its pure blue flowers on arching stems throughout autumn.

Another good autumn blue, dense violet really, is *Liriope muscari*, a grassy-leaved member of the lily family and a close relation of the black grass, *Ophiopogon*. If you're interested in mixing your blues with a shocking pink, *Liriope* has enough red in it to allow it associate harmlessly with the hardy *Nerine bowdenii*, which flowers at the same time.

For a splash of red, the upright, dark-leaved *Lobelia cardinalis* 'Queen Victoria', red penstemons, good red dahlias such as 'The Bishop of Llandaff', shrubby small-leaved red salvias from Mexico (cuttings taken now are easy and advisable, as these are not always hardy), *Crocosmia* 'Lucifer' and the South American kaffir lily, *Schizostylis coccinea*, are all good things to garner for the autumn garden.

My own *Schizostylis* have become so overcrowded that I started dividing some only two weeks ago, even though they're due to start flowering any minute now. They've taken to their new homes and are doing as well, if not better, than those remaining in the congested clumps. Certainly they're fatter, and though they're unlikely to flower now, I'm hoping they'll put out for November and even December, if the weather stays mild.

Right now my favourite thing in the garden is the coolest-looking 'red hot poker' I've yet seen. A jewel in jade and white, *Kniphofia* 'Green Jade' has given me a flower (one) for the first time. The two-year wait has been worth it. The flower head is six or seven inches long and the four-foot stem so stout that it has remained standing, impervious to attack from slugs and snails, which sadly defeated the earlier *Kniphofia*, 'Samuel's Sensation'.

September

There is a flurry of activity in the affairs of gardeners now, with to do before the leaves fall in earnest and the big sweep be Perennials and biennials grown from seed have to be moved to permanent place in the garden, or potted on to give to friends. D heading and cutting back should continue apace. Fruit has t picked, potatoes lifted and stored away from the light. Spinach be sown for an early crop in April – real spinach that doesn't coat teeth unpleasantly like some of the perpetual beet spinaches. La like to be aerated now, a physically demanding job. Spike with a f or a customized spiker, then dress the wounds with a mixture of co post and horticultural sand.

Seeds of annual poppies, larkspur, marigold, cornflower, clar and blue nigella (Love-in-a-Mist) can all be sown outside now, in t places you want them to flower. Thinning out can be left until sprin Gales and strong gusts of wind are part of the September landscap Vulnerable new growth on climbers should be loosely tied in wit soft twine. Allow enough to accommodate thickening stems.

Long shoots growing from ground level on roses or other climber can be bent over into arching shapes to encourage flowering buds t break along their length. If you have good, strong iron railing around your house, try weaving a vigorous climbing or rambling ros through it. A virtual wall of blossom will reward your efforts.

Spent summer bedding has to be lifted and composted to make room for wallflowers and spring bulbs. Wallflowers grown from seed are best, usually stronger and in the colour you want. If buying plants, choose sturdy, not leggy, ones that have had the tips pinched out to make them bushy. If your local nursery doesn't do wallflowers in groups of one colour, ask them why not.

But the most urgent task in September is getting spring bulbs into

ural and essential feed which sustains the flowered bulbs and nourishes them for next year.

Hardy geraniums are early and good for taking over from bulbs. Hellebores, particularly, are good planted with snowdrops and snowflakes, which come up prettily between their strongly defined leaves. Crocus are another joy of early spring and some of the species are easy to naturalize in grass. *Crocus vernus*, the origin of the large purple Dutch crocus, is a marvellous spreader. There is a white form, *albiflorus*, but it's less easy. Good for grass or well-drained soil is another species crocus, a spreader by seed, *C. tommasinianus*. Its leaves are narrow, and its fleeting flowers, pale purple lit by a distinctive white tube, will lift their heads to flower through late winter snow.

༄

Hyacinth bulbs for Christmas (sorry to mention that word in September) should be started off now in a dark cupboard, at about 48 degrees Fahrenheit. Unwin's bulb catalogue lists 'Carnegie', which it says needs eleven weeks in the dark, followed by three in the light, and also 'Blue Delft', which comes on faster, needing only nine weeks of darkness and twenty-three days of light. But take care, as hyacinth bulbs can irritate the skin. Don't neglect to pot up at least a dozen bulbs of the heavenly paperwhite narcissus as well.

༄

When flowering is over, prune old stems of well-established rambling roses down to their base, and ditto with the spent canes on autumn-fruiting raspberries.

༄

Stake tall asters, dahlias, heleniums and other autumn flowers as discreetly as possible. It's best to do this earlier in the season, while the plants are still small. They might look obtrusive at first, but the plants will soon fill out to obscure them.

༄

Early apples, such as Discovery, should be picked as soon as the stems part easily from the branches. Victoria plums are ready for eating when the wasps begin to pay them a lot of attention. A day on the kitchen windowsill will further sweeten any picked a tad too soon.

❧

Some herbs can be propagated now. Take cuttings of thyme by pulling off virile shoots and pushing them into the ground around their parent, where they should take root in about four weeks. Rosemary will suffer the same treatment, or can be potted up, along with lavender and sage, in a loose compost. Sage can also be layered: take a sappy branch and nick along it near a leaf node, then peg it down into the soil, still attached to the parent. Cover it with a sprinkling of soil, and water.

❧

Rooted bits of mint, chive, oregano, marjoram and whole parsley and basil plants can be gently dug up and potted for winter use indoors.

❧

Except in very cold and wet areas where planting should be left until spring, autumn is the best time to plant garlic, for cropping next July and August. Choose a variety bred for the climate rather than using left-over kitchen cloves that probably came from much warmer climates. Plant single cloves in well-drained soil, with the pointed tip just showing above the earth. Garlic is said to be a good companion for roses because aphids steer well clear.

❧

Look at your roses carefully. Pick any leaves showing signs of blackspot and mildew and burn them. Don't leave them where they fall or use in making compost or they'll spread their diseases. Prune weak or damaged stems down to the ground.

❧

If planting winter pansies as bedding, remember that winter growth will be slow, so pack them closely together for the best effect. Tulips can be planted in between for later spring interest.

∾

Hardy *Cyclamen hederifolium* are flowering at full tilt now, a miraculous sight in autumn when all is falling dead around them. The amazingly delicate-looking flowers appear first and are later joined by beautifully marked foliage that resembles particularly elegant ivy. If you are without, admire them elsewhere and resolve to have them next year. But please check before you buy that they haven't been plundered from their wild native habitats. Usually pink, they look remarkably fresh surrounded by autumn leaves. Self-sown seedlings often come up pure white.

∾

If busy-lizzies and begonias are still in good nick outdoors, you could pot some up for bringing indoors, keeping a big rootball and adding some fresh compost. Petunias can also be brought indoors. Cut them hard back before potting up and they should eventually give a fresh flush of flowers.

∾

Except for those seedheads you want to leave for decoration or drying, deadhead everything in sight, annuals and perennials, to extend their flowering period. Cut back to the base of the flower stalk at least, to ensure there are no ungainly, headless stems sticking out.

∾

If you haven't already, then do give the scalloped-leaved Lady's Mantle, *Alchemilla mollis*, the chop after its airy, lime-green flowers have faded. A fresh crop of pretty foliage will appear from the base to grace the late autumn garden.

∾

Trim hedges of box, yew, privet, beech and laurel. Prune those rambling and climbing roses that have only one flush of flowers. Encourage new wood to sprout from the base by cutting out old wood entirely. Otherwise, a good yardstick for pruning is: cut back the same amount of old growth as there is new growth to make up for it.

∾

Basal-rooting lilies, i.e. most lilies of European and some of American origin, are best planted in autumn for growing in pots.

∾

In the warmer counties (that's most of them) a spring lettuce crop can be sown to overwinter without protection. Arctic King and Winter Density are suitable for this treatment. Planting should be done by early October. Parsley seed can be sown outside now for using in spring.

October

An autumnal feel has crept up almost without our noticing. Suddenly we're ankle-deep in leaves and the garden's scent is strong, bitter-sweet, its colours softening towards decay. Mellow yellows, reds and pinks set the background tone for great bursts of new colour from dahlias, asters, sedums, penstemons, late geraniums and roses.

Cool, elegant and tall, the annual white cosmos, grown from seed sown in early summer, shows no sign of fatigue and has bulked out nicely to fill the spaces where the Japanese anemone hybrid, *A.* 'Honorine Jobert', will flower next year. Hybrid anemones take a while to settle in to new quarters, but then spread quickly even in shade, giving masses of fresh white or rose-pink flowers for nearly three months. Hardy nerines (*Nerine bowdenii*), slightly shocking in their pinkness and best against a warm, well-drained wall, are coming on stream, while naked ladies, also known as autumn crocus (*Colchicum*), and red kaffir lilies (*Schizostylis coccinea*) are queuing to take their turn.

October is a golden time to work in the garden. Soft-lit days are warm, slow and still, while all around you deciduous leaves are colouring-up in preparation for a final autumn fling. The soil is lovely to dig – warm, moist and receptive after September's rain. It's perfect for moving and dividing perennials, changing plants around to suit your tastes while you can still see the shape and size of them, and remember their colour. You can do all that in spring, but the plants have a head start if they get their roots down now. Compacted fallow ground should be dug over deeply – two spits – and left lying in big ignorant clods. Winter frosts will break them down into fine particles of soil, ready for enriching and planting next year.

October is the last month in which you can safely plant ever-greens. Deciduous and fruit trees can be planted any time from now until Christmas. Prepare the planting site well at least a week in advance, digging the hole deep and wide and incorporating plenty of organic material, plus potash if you're planting fruit. If using manure, make sure it is buried under a layer of earth at the bottom of the planting hole and is not touching the young roots. Stake all trees at planting time to hold them steady against the wind.

There's still time to sow or lay a new lawn. Make sure the chosen site is weed-free and finely raked. Water in dry weather until established and try not to walk it into a mush during winter.

If outdoor tomatoes show any sign of pink this month, it's safer to bring them indoors, still clinging to their vines, to ripen on a sunny windowsill. Those that will obviously never ripen can be made into a green tomato chutney, which complements Indian dishes. Small, early spring bulbs should already be in, and every other bulb you have, or want to have, should go in as soon as possible. Tulips are an exception: I've put them in as late as December and they've come up at the same time as identical types planted earlier.

Small spring bulbs are good when planting windowboxes and pots for winter interest. Winter pansies are amazing, the way they keep going unrattled all winter, but they only last one season. Delicate, trailing ivies make a good foil for bulbs and a young, upright Miss Jessop rosemary, or a small, clipped evergreen (bay, box, yew) or perhaps a blueish dwarf conifer, will add structure and balance to a windowbox or other container.

And then there's the falling leaves, coming thicker and faster the more you try to clear them. I know some people can't bear an untidy garden and feel tense and upset until they remove every bit of sagging foliage from herbaceous plants; whether the plant can survive the winter without its cloak of decay is academic to them. Or they might like to spend their time gathering every leaf as it falls onto the border, path or grass. If leaves are not smothering delicate, light-loving or slug-prone plants, the last fall of leaves can be left in the borders. Under trees and shrubs and larger herbaceous stuff, they give some protection till spring. Any leaves the worms don't pull underground to make humus, can be cleared away from young shoots in spring.

But hard surfaces are another thing. Even the most laid-back gardener can feel swamped as leaves fill up every corner of yard, terrace or beds. A good sweep of hard surfaces about once a week is deeply rewarding, satisfying the dictates of the work ethic and the pleasure principle in one go. Forgotten spaces reclaimed from chaos give you breathing space before tackling the next job, and make the place seem bigger and more promising.

Free caviar for your pet plants can be made from fallen leaves. Leafmould is pure and simple and excellent for mixing into special potting compost. Most often, it's made in a specially constructed, chicken-wire cage, where it takes two to three years to rot down, depending on the type of (deciduous) leaf. A thick black plastic sack is quicker and more compact where space is limited. Fill with wet leaves, tie, pierce with a fork or toothpick and hide it away in a damp place for eighteen months or so.

Use the last grass cuttings of the year as a handy mulch around needy plants, remembering that there's little point in mulching on dry ground. Yes, the odd bit of grass may take root *in situ*, but it will be easier to pull and less harmful than the weeds it will smother.

November

Late autumn is really the beginning of the gardening year, not the end, despite so many signs to the contrary. It's the time to make plans and adjustments, time for the great tidy-up that is rewarded by sightings of the first spring bulbs. By now, most of the leaves are down and the grass is waiting for its final haircut before winter. Twigs and branches of all shapes, colours and sizes are lying all over the place. The long hot summer yielded bushels of walnuts from my nearest city park. Blackberries were plentiful for jam and horse chestnuts have been soaked in malt vinegar and left in the hot-press to go hard as iron, the time-honoured way to make the best fighting conkers.

What bounty. So I was suprised when a friend, who lives on an old, tree-lined road in Dublin, rang me to complain about the huge ash branch that had broken off in his garden, and the thick carpet of fallen leaves he was going to have to bag for the bin or burn. The ash branch was so big, he was going to have to pay a fortune for a skip to take it away. This friend uses firelighters, buys all his composts expensively bagged and even buys bunches of twigs in Habitat (yes twigs, imported twigs) to decorate his pretty house and gather dust.

Now he has been persuaded that to burn or dump leaves is not only a sin against nature, it's looking a gift horse in the mouth. Like so many city gardeners, he has no compost bin, no wire net cage for rotting down leaves into crumbly leafmould. So instead, on my advice, he stuffed the leaves tight into strong plastic sacks, quickly tied and then pierced in a few places with a fork. They are now tucked out of sight at the bottom of his garden for the next year or two, which is how long it takes them to rot down. Beech and oak rot faster, plane and sycamore take longer. Leathery evergreen should not be used and pine needles are too acid. Good compost can be made in the same way with grass, soft-stemmed clippings, garden debris and vegetable waste.

The huge ash branch has now been cut up and stacked for logs and the twiggy bits tied into artistic bundles to make kindling for winter fires. He's feeling proud and righteous, much richer in purse and clearer of conscience. He is now to be seen roaming the streets of his district in search of more leaves and fallen branches. A word of warning, though, to the serious asthmatic: compost heaps or any garden moulds can bring on an attack and should be avoided. So too should most grasses and any daisy-like flowers.

There is still plenty of time left to plant tulips. From now until December (and even later, in my experience) the bulbs can be bedded out or planted in pots. Either way, give them plenty of sharp drainage, that is, garden sand or grit added to the compost – never use builder's sand, as it contains salts, clogs the soil and causes rot. In pots you can plant different bulbs in layers to flower at different times. The general rule for this method is the bigger the bulb, the deeper it goes – say double its own depth, in a good, rich mixture of loam-based compost. Liquid feeding during flowering is beneficial.

Most tulips die away in the ground after a few years, the flowers getting smaller until they just disappear altogether. I've been lucky with some old, tall scarlet and flame ones which I got from a next-door neighbour who was discarding them. If anything, they have multiplied, even though planted in unworked, heavy clay seven years ago. Having just acquired a large bag of White Triumphators, my hopes are running high. Not only are they a glowing white, tall and lily-shaped, but Christopher Lloyd claims that they have actually increased while bedded out in his garden at Dixter. They also look striking massed in large elegant clay pots.

If you were prudent enough to take pelargonium cuttings in summer, pot them up now to make good roots for next year. Garlic should be planted now. Take a good, firm head, from the kitchen store if necessary, separate it into cloves and plant in lightish, well-drained soil in sun. Homegrown garlic is juicy and almost sweet, though usually the heads are smaller than their counterparts from hotter countries. Windowboxes need clearing and can be made ready for a new display – maybe winter pansies, variegated ivies, irises (*unguicularis* flowers from December), crocuses and snowdrops.

If you're exhausted after all that, put your feet up and fantasize by the fire with the seed catalogues. Some can be had from garden stockists, others have to be ordered. Ads for these appear regularly in periodicals. But beware of their descriptions ('seeds itself about' means it's usually a nuisance, for example, but that's useful in new, barely furnished gardens) and learn to read between the lines.

∾

Prepare ground for planting shrubs, trees and roses later in the autumn. The same applies if you plan on moving them about.

∾

You can cut down and compost any herbaceous foliage now, if you like, but not penstemons. They're not fully hardy, so leave their foliage on till spring to protect them from frost.

∾

Lots of herbaceous stuff, such as geraniums and hostas, can be cut or divided now, to increase your stock and give them new life. But leave the late flowerers – crocosmia, aster, and ornamental grasses – until spring.

∾

Hand-weed new weed seedlings, even for five minutes a day, to stop them getting too comfortable and established.

∾

You can plant winter heathers now. *Erica carnea*, famous for its (very late) winter flowering, is an exception in that it doesn't need acid soil. Sweet and alkaline will do fine.

∾

To lift or not to lift your dahlias for the winter, that is the question. The answer is, it depends on where you live, what type of soil they're in, how many you've got and how much you would miss them if they were killed by frost. Very heavy wet clay is not their idea of a good time, but in well-drained soil in milder parts of the country it's usually safe enough to leave them where they lie.

ॐ

Sloe gin is traditionally made in early November for drinking at Christmas the following year (if you can't resist drinking it, try keeping a small jar for the full year and taste the astonishing difference). Here's a simple recipe: First collect your sloes and for every pound, use six ounces of sugar and loads of gin. Take a wide-necked jar with a screw-on lid, maybe a kilner jar. Prick the sloes all over and cram them into the jar in layers, sprinkling sugar between each layer. When the jar is full, top it up to the brim with gin.

Keep doing this until the sloes, or gin, have been used up. Screw the lid on tightly and leave in a dark place until you hear its little voice calling 'drink me, drink me', just over a year from now. Obey the voice and strain it into clean bottles for drinking.

ॐ

Cut back mallows to the quick if they've finished flowering and are just an ungainly mess. New growth will spring from the base next year.

ॐ

The 25th of November is St Catherine's Day in France. Tradition there says it's the best day of the year to plant trees, including fruit trees. If you are going to put down a tree of some sort, try to prepare the hole a bit in advance to let it settle, making it one-third wider than the tree's root system. Break up the bottom layer of soil, incorporating grit if it needs help in draining and mixing in plenty of organic matter. If manure is being used, cover it with a good layer of soil or the acid in it will burn the roots if there is direct contact.

Firm and slightly mound the base of the hole. Put a strong stake in first, about three inches from the centre to allow for the tree's future expansion and prevent it from being uprooted by winter gales before it's established. Plant firmly with the visible soil mark at ground level, which is the same depth at which it was growing in the nursery beds, or container if a potted specimen. Soak the roots really well before planting.

Backfill the hole in stages while another person holds the tree upright. Shake it gently from time to time as you go along to settle the soil between the roots. Keep firming it in and when the hole is nearly full, break up the soil around the edges and stamp on it all, to give firmness over a bigger area. Use something soft and pliable to bind the tree to its stake, but make sure it's cushioned and can't chafe the tender young bark of the tree.

Old bicycle tubes, looped and tied in a figure of eight between the tree and the stake, work well, or you can buy specially made ties. Even if you live in the city and don't have to worry about rabbits and deer, cats and dogs can do a lot of damage to a tree's trunk, making wounds where disease can enter during the winter. A piece of chicken wire, or a palisade of viciously thorny rose prunings surrounding the stem, stops them scratching and tearing at it. Finish with an organic mulch and a few shovelfuls of potash from the bonfire mixed in lightly.

∾

Lilies can still be planted out for next year if the ground is still easily worked, or in pots where you can ensure the best conditions for them. Above all else, lilies demand good drainage, so incorporate plenty of horticultural sand or grit into the planting mix and a layer at the bottom of their planting holes.

∾

Though roots virtually stop growing in winter, autumn-planted evergreens can be kept growing if given a thick mulch now. They can be frustratingly slow to put on growth but the mulch will give them a head start and by spring they should be noticeably larger.

❧

If you live in a very cold area, it's wiser to leave some foliage on summer-flowering perennials to protect their crowns from frost. Otherwise, it's a good time to move and divide them if they're congested, in the wrong place or you wish to increase your stock. If dividing, discard the central woody bit and replant the more vigorous pieces with roots, taken from around the edges.

❧

Turf lawns can still be laid. They arrive in strips rolled up like stair carpet. Rake the soil to a fine, level tilth, removing any larger stones and all weeds. The supplier will advise you on laying technique. It is important to pack the edges of the turves or strips tightly side by side, almost but not quite overlapping, so that they can knit seamlessly. Water if the weather is dry and try to avoid walking on it until it has rooted.

❧

Rearrange your pots outside, tucking those that are spent or unsightly out of the way and dragging anything presentable into the limelight, where it can be seen from the windows of the house. It's handy to have a few evergreens, including ivies underplanted with bulbs, permanently in pots for this very purpose.

❧

Grape vines, honeysuckle, wisteria and other deciduous climbers can be pruned now but not those that flower in spring, such as *Clematis montana, C. alpina*, or the Japanese quinces, *Chaenomeles*, which have been flowering for weeks already in the Botanic Gardens in Glasnevin.

❧

Check that emerging bulbs and plants with good winter foliage, such as *Pulmonaria* (Lungwort), are clear of leaves, which deprive them of the light they need for growing, as well as harbouring hordes of slugs and snails.

∾

Although the major pruning of roses is best left until spring, long growths on an established bush can be pruned back to about thirty inches to prevent wind damage. Use only a very sharp secateurs. A snaggly, torn cut is more likely to attract disease.

December

Now is when the panic sets in. Winter is here and gardeners' thoughts
are turning to the dark months ahead when pleasures are few. Will
the garden put out any surprises in December, the bleakest month –
maybe a branch of scented *Viburnum fragrans* for the house, or cheerful berries for Christmas?

If the prospect from now until spring is really bleak, you could
decide not to cut down existing mixed borders at all this winter, leaving architectural shapes and rounded mass to make a brittle but interesting picture, particularly when gripped by frost. If the border is
backed by a dark evergreen hedge, the effect is even better.

Winter scents are precious and not so few. A good plan is to have
scented plants near the doors of the house. Their lavish fragrance will
lift your heart every time you step in or out, and they'll glory in the
shelter that the house provides. Sweet-scented *Viburnum farreri* (*V.
fragrans*) has blush-white, apple-blossom flowers that start opening
in November and, unless halted by unusually severe frosts, will keep
going until March.

An extremely hardy shrub, aptly dubbed the Fragrant Guelder, *V.
farreri* likes a moist enough soil, and needs sunshine to set its buds
well. Eventually reaching a height of ten or twelve feet, it smells particularly sweet when cut and brought into a warm room, but should
be left out in the cold at night if it's to last any length indoors. There
are other good viburnums: *V. Bodnantense* 'Dawn', which is as long-
flowering as *V. farreri*, but not quite so beautiful, though it does last
longer as a cut flower. *V. x burkwoodii* is classed as an evergreen in
milder parts and flowers twice, once in October–November and
again in April–May.

Wintersweet (*Chimonanthus praecox*) is not famous for its looks,
though the form 'Luteus' has broader petals of light yellow than the

species, if not quite as good a scent, and can be wall-trained. Wintersweets need all the sun they can get to ripen their twiggy, greyish wood and will flower well on poorish ground with a western aspect. Two honeysuckles give good scent in winter, *Lonicera standishii* and *L. fragrantissima*, both bushy shrubs to a height of six feet with small, cream flowers about an inch all round. A probable hybrid of these two, *L. x purpusii*, is regarded as having the better qualities of both parents.

Winter jasmine, the yellow *Jasminum nudiflorum* – nude because its starry flowers bloom on stiff, cascading naked branches – is not scented at all, but no winter garden should be without one. Not fussy as to soil or shade, it can even be grown in a pot, and can start flowering in October and not stop until April. Branches in bud brought into the house open slowly and last for ages.

Clematis cirrhosa balearica is a true winter-flowering climber from the Balearic Islands, with neat, finely cut, glossy dark foliage. The flowers are creamy-green bells splashed inside with tiny, mahogany marks. For the warmest counties only, or a cold greenhouse, *Clematis nepaulensis* (or *C. forrestii*), from northern India and neighbouring parts of China, opens its creamy flowers with purple stamens from December onwards.

Cornus, the willow or dogwood, is renowned for the dramatic impact of its brightly coloured stems in deepest winter. *Cornus alba*, with pearly berries, is amazing reflected in water. *C. sibirica* is a compact variety more suited to smaller gardens, with good autumn colour and brilliant red bark. Bark comes into its own in the winter and many of the maples, particularly the paperbark and snakebark acers, are lovely and can stand alone as a focal point.

The heart surgeon Maurice Neligan once wrote a letter to the *Irish Times* extolling the virtues of our native strawberry tree, *Arbutus unedo*. Unfortunately, I can't find the piece to quote from it, but he made a convincing case for this compact, evergreen tree, which has attractive, burnt red bark and winter flowers that appear simultaneously with the strawberry-shaped fruits. *A. andrachnoides* has vivid, red-brown bark.

Down at ground level, there are the old friends – early crocuses, cyclamen and snowdrops – but not many people seem to know about the winter aconites (*Eranthis hiemalis*) which, if they establish, will pop their bright, buttercup heads and fresh green little ruffs four inches above the snow in January and February. Nor does the Algerian Iris (*I. unguicularis*, formerly *I. stylosa*) enjoy the fame it deserves, especially as a scented cut flower. It blooms on and off from autumn until April and should be planted where the sun can bake it in summer. Keep an eye out for slugs, which like it well enough, and remove browning, messy foliage which only hides the beggars.

The hellebores are a large family of winter-flowering herbaceous plants, with good sculptural qualities and plenty of poise. *H. niger*, the Christmas Rose, starts the show with pure white blooms from late November. Camellias can flower for Christmas in warm sites, kaffir lilies will flame until the first hard frosts, and the crab, *Malus 'Robustus'*, a pleasing tree to twenty feet, will keep its crimson, cherry-size fruits until well into the new year.

∽

After the ground has had its first taste of frost, you may wonder if it's safe to keep digging and planting. Planting is fine, but not when the ground is actually frozen. Wait for the thaw between frosts. Digging any patches of bare earth can only be beneficial now, if the soil is not waterlogged. By exposing the topsoil, pests and weed seeds are killed off and heavier clays are broken down into a friable tilth.

∽

If a plant is frozen in its pot don't plunge it into hot water to thaw – this will almost certainly kill it. A bucket of cold water will do. Sprinkle the foliage with cold water and stand the pot in a cool place that is properly frostproof, out of sunshine. When it has thawed, which takes several hours, move to a warmer atmosphere.

∽

Check any bulbs you have potted up for forcing early indoors, such as hyacinths and narcissi. The compost should not be dry, nor soggy. Just damp.

∾

Some Christmas trees, like the Norway spruce, shed their needles shamelessly. Others, like the Noble and Nordmann fir, keep their finery better. But none of them really like the dryness of central heating. If your tree has already been cut, you should take a further inch off the stem and leave it outdoors in a container of water. A few days before Christmas, pot it up in a large container filled with garden soil, or use a stand with a water tray. Keep the soil moist, or the water topped up, and the tree away from direct heat. This should keep it looking good until it lives out its traditional welcome on the 6th of January, the Christian feast of the Epiphany.

∾

Think about getting a weather vane made. They are lovely things, and at least you'll know which way the wind is blowing.

∾

Plant tulips. If not in pots, then try to put them where their dying stalks will be hidden by burgeoning perennials after they have flowered. If the ground is heavy, break it up with plenty of gritty stuff and plant them deep – three times their own depth if possible. That way their stalks will be longer and stronger.

∾

Many imported clay pots are made in Italy and Spain and are not fully frostproof. If you live in a frosty area, the pots can crack when the moisture in the soil freezes and expands. Take them out of their saucers now and let them drain freely by standing them on evenly balanced little legs, made of anything you have to hand, or buy those pretty lion's paws made specially for the job. In a very bad winter you'll have to wrap the pots in some insulating material, tie them in the middle and pretend you don't see them.

❧

Remember to dig those holes for tree planting in advance. If cutting holes in established lawns, save the turf and place it grass-side down in the bottom of the hole. It will rot and provide improving humus for the soil.

❧

If you decide to feed the birds this winter, it's best to realize that it's a long-term commitment. Birds will travel for miles if they hear there's food going, so if you forget to leave some out they will have wasted their reserves of precious energy for nothing. If you're encouraging wildlife, particularly around a pond, it's better not to be too

tidy about that area. Leave plenty of cover for small mammals – leaves and shrubby undergrowth – where they can sleep and find essential food such as woodlice, snails and slugs.

∾

Bare-rooted plants – roses, hedging, fruit and other trees – are cheaper than potted ones and come into their own now. Dig in plenty of rich compost when planting for surer rewards next year.

∾

Alpine plants love good drainage and can't bear having a wet collar of leaves around their necks. Clear away debris and any lower decaying leaves, and hand-weed between them.

∾

Wash seed trays and pots in soapy water before the muck gets too caked and stubborn. It will save you time and work in the busy spring rush, when everything will start screaming for attention.

∾

If you are making a bonfire of uncompostable or diseased material, move it to a fresh site first to ensure there are no small creatures (slug-swilling hedgehogs if you are lucky) nesting snugly beneath it.

∾

Evergreens in pots should be moved to a sheltered position for the worst of the winter. It is bad for their health if the soil and roots are allowed to freeze. If frost is very bad, then wrapping them in hessian, a special fleece, or even bubblewrap if you can bear to look at it, will insulate them against the worst the weather can offer.

∾

Now that the leaves are down, it's a good time to see if wires and ties on climbers need securing against high winds. It is also a good time to start building walls and paths.

❧

Prune autumn-fruiting raspberries down to the ground, and grape-vines when they've lost all their leaves and before the sap starts to flow again early next year. Cut back all the vine's sideshoots to within one or two buds of the main stem.

❧

Roses can be pruned between now and early spring, though the latter is safer in very cold areas. If planting roses, do so when the soil is dry or just moist, but never if it's wet and sticky or has frost or snow on the surface. Firm in well around the roots and use plenty of mulch on the surface.

❧

When flower buds are showing through, bring pots of bulbs into the warmth and keep them moist. Move house-plants away from freezing-cold windowsills at night. Life is hard behind the curtains.

Index